The Enquiring Tutor

The Enquiring Tutor:
Exploring the Process of Professional Learning

Stephen Rowland

 The Falmer Press

(A member of the Taylor & Francis Group)
London · Washington, D.C.

UK   The Falmer Press, 4 John Street, London WC1N 2ET
USA   The Falmer Press, Taylor & Francis Inc., 1900 Frost Road, Suite 101, Bristol, PA 19007

First published 1993

A catalogue record for this book is available from the British Library

Library of Congress Cataloging-in-Publication Data are available on request

ISBN 0 75070 210 9
ISBN 0 75070 211 7 (paper)

Jacket design by Caroline Archer

Typeset in 11/13pt Bembo
by Graphicraft Typesetters Ltd., Hong Kong.

Printed in Great Britain by Burgess Science Press, Basingstoke on paper which has a specified pH value on final paper manufacture of not less than 7.5 and is therefore 'acid free'.

Contents

Acknowledgments

I would like to thank the people I have worked with who have allowed me to use extracts from their writings in this book. My relationship with them has formally been one of tutor to student. But many have become friends and colleagues as we have begun to understand each other's professional enthusiasms and explore the personal values which underly our work. Kath Bailey, Ray Bancroft, Liz Benson, Adrienne Buchanan, Suzanne Clegg, Sarah Cooke, Alison Duncan, Ellen Gascoigne, Richard Hall, Ruth Gallagher, Aisha Henry, Jeanne Keay, Theresa Langfield, Jill Moore, Andy Patterson, David Roberts, Ivy Taylor and Pauline Williams have all contributed in this way. As well as letting me use their own words in the development of my story, and helping me to edit parts of the text, I am grateful to them for the many conversations which have helped me to understand the significance of their experience on courses which I have run. I hope that I have portrayed their feelings and thoughts faithfully.

I also want to thank Neil Bolton for generously permitting me to present a somewhat unfair caricature of his position in the introduction. I have always valued his thoughtfulness, encouragement and humour. Many other colleagues in the Division of Education at the University of Sheffield have helped me to work through these ideas at a time when we have to struggle to protect the space for thought from the business demands of academic life.

Finally, I don't think I could have written this book without the help of Gillie Bolton. Her enthusiasm, gentle criticism and insight have been a continual source of inspiration at every stage of the journey. She has always helped me to make the move from familiar ground onto the more uncertain territory of fresh ideas. My story owes much to her partnership in the struggle to make sense of our working lives.

Chapter 1

Introduction

Fieldnote

Andrew and Ann are two experienced teachers who are students on our Masters course. Yesterday they came to talk to me, as their tutor counsellor, after their first seminar with a colleague of mine. As soon as they came in I thought that they looked uneasy, as if they had something difficult to say. I asked them how the first session had gone.

Andrew was the first to speak: 'I didn't understand half of what he was saying. I think that's appalling. He should be able to say it in a way we can understand.'

'How did you feel, Ann? Did you understand what was going on?'

'Well, most of it, not really, it was a bit beyond me.'

'So did you mind not really understanding it?'

'Oh no! I don't know much about psychology, I can't be expected to understand much of what it was about. I daresay I'll pick it up as we go along, but just now I let most of it go above my head.'

'But that's no good', Andrew chipped in, 'You've got a right to demand that the lecturer make himself clear to you. It's no good just accepting all this jargon — he shouldn't be allowed to get away with it. We wouldn't expect to get away with it at school. As teachers it's our job to make ourselves clear to the kids. In the same way, it's the lecturer's job to make himself clear to us.'

Andrew and Ann had had quite different expectations about what a higher education course in professional development would be like. Andrew talked of his 'rights', Ann's expectations were based upon her sense of her own ignorance. I wondered how their lecturer felt about the session.

Neil is a close colleague of mine, with many more years experi-ence in higher education than I. I respect his work as a psychologist and he is someone I can talk to. Nevertheless, I felt uneasy about bringing this conversation to his attention. It could seem as though I were being critical of his teaching. So when he joined me for coffee this morning I wanted to broach the topic of my conversation with Ann and Andrew gently.

'Did you feel the students were clear about what you were saying in that seminar?' A far from gentle opening.

'Well I try to put these ideas into everyday language', Neil replied, 'but you can only do that up to a certain point. In the end it's up to the students whether or not they learn from what I've got to say. I'm like a resource they can use. I express my ideas and my commit-ment to the subject matter through what I say, but I can't determine what they take away from it. They can ask me questions, and I'll try to answer them to the best of my ability. But in the end it's not up to me what they learn — if they learn — that's up to them. I'm not too interested in pedagogy. We're not here to spoon feed the students. They work alongside us — learn from us — if they will. More a kind of master-apprentice relationship than that of a teacher and child.'

Differences of View

Neil, Andrew and Ann appear to have quite different views about the relationship between the adult professional learner, tutor and subject matter. Both Neil and Andrew compare their engagement in higher education with their experience in school. For Andrew, a teacher with several years experience, the responsibilities of a professional tutor are the same as those for a school teacher. Neil is an academic and peda-gogy is not his prime concern. It is not his responsibility to motivate his students or to check up that they understand at every stage. They are adults now. If they have a problem they can ask and he will do his best to explain. But it's their responsibility to ask. Whether or not Ann accepts this as her responsibility is not clear, but it is not one she exercises: in spite of not understanding her lecturer, she doesn't ask him to explain, hoping she will pick it up as things progress.

This book is an exploration of this kind of relationship and its dynamic within the social context in which it arises. I shall be concerned with the *processes* of learning, rather than with the details of *what* pro-fessional teachers, nurses or social workers should be taught and learn on professional courses. Although I shall address questions concerning the content of professional learning, the enquiry is not content specific.

Educational processes are elusive. Rarely can we look at an event or an experience and say: 'that was learning'. There are moments when 'the penny drops', but these are the exceptions. Learning normally takes place without us being fully aware of what we are learning, or how. Some approaches to educational and psychological investigation have attempted to reduce the complexity of learning to categories (such as cognitive and affective learning) or to stages (such as concrete and formal), or to identify the particular skills involved in learning. But such attempts make little impact upon how we think of ourselves as learners and teachers of those with whom we engage. An adequate theory of learning would have to be one which explained all human interaction if not the very process of living itself.

Listening to the Students

A starting point, however, seems to be to listen to our students. This can be uncomfortable at times. With Andrew and Ann that was not much of a problem for me: it was a colleague's practice that was being criticized, not mine. In this next illustration from my fieldnotes, I was the one under attack.

Fieldnote

It is a month now since I ran the four-day residential course. I had deliberately kept the agenda on this course open and had tried to be 'non-directive' in the way I handled the course, hoping that the issues would emerge from the participants' professional practice rather than directly from my concerns. Most of the participants have now written to me as part of their course evaluation, saying how they felt about the course, what they learnt and so on. Today I received a letter from Alison. I had not been aware that she had been unhappy with the course. Here are some extracts from her letter:

I experienced excruciating boredom when we all sat round in a circle, verbalizing: meaningful communication seemed to be achieved too rarely. I also felt frustration at the torpid inactivity of this fabricated hothouse atmosphere. It was the irritation of the inertia which led to outbursts, impatience, confrontation. The justification that these were natural insecurities and hostilities which needed to be externalized in order to be resolved seems to me inadequate. Rather than generating such Strindbergian angst, it would have been better to find (or, indeed, initially to be offered) channels through which such rampant energy could be better directed. Harmony and cooperation emerged whenever we were in small groups, involved in a particular activity, suggesting that people get on better when doing rather than when talking. Words take up time, they can act as diversions, blocking and hampering; actions seem to have greater precision . . .

. . . All of us in the group were, from the first moment, effectively de-skilled, at one stroke. Little attention was paid to the skills, talents, experiences of life that we brought with us. In effect we were denuded of our positive qualities, and sat around in that circle as flawed human beings and only that. I think that this abrupt stripping us of any good feelings about ourselves led to much hostility.

Four pages of angry yet articulate response was only relieved in the last paragraph by this sentence:

. . . Yet I have good memories of the course because of my experience of getting to like very much the other members of the group . . .

My reaction on reading this letter was confused. So much of the way she wrote seemed to reflect my own values. I could not just dismiss her as a student who was not up to the course or whose values were in such opposition to mine that she was bound to have a bad experience. I had even thought I quite liked her. She had appeared sensitive and thoughtful on the course. Yet her feelings, not reflected in the letters from the other participants, were so hostile. What was wrong?

Talking this over with a colleague I can remember defending myself. I reasoned that Alison had not been prepared to confront her own personal difficulties with the group. She was refusing to take any responsibility for the interaction that had taken place. Since the other participants had not shared her feelings, perhaps she was just an unfortunate exception. Perhaps with more time she would come to see the value of the experience. She admitted that she ended up feeling good about the other participants. Since the course aimed to be a team building exercise, it would appear that this aim had been met for her even if she couldn't admit it because she didn't like the process.

All these justifications and explanations helped me to defend myself from Alison's criticisms. But if I was to learn from her letter, I would need to stop blaming her, to listen more carefully, and to realize my own responsibilities. This would be uncomfortable.

So many questions were raised by Alison's letter. They concerned not only my technical abilities as a tutor — my skill — but, more significantly, ethical issues underlying my practice. What was my responsibility in organizing an experience which turned out to be painful for her, and what was hers? Was I obliged to provide a 'safe' atmosphere for learning? Was she or was I in a better position to judge the value of her experience?

It may seem odd to start a book about learning, with two instances of what appear to be failure (although not unique, John Holt wrote a very influential book on *How Children Fail* (1965) (before he wrote a somewhat less inspiring book on *How Children Learn*) (1967)). Why begin with failure?

First, I could only begin to improve my practice as a tutor once I had faced my own sense of failure. We all fail at times, and these occasions can become valuable points of growth in our own development.

Secondly, it is not easy to elicit genuine evaluative comments from course participants. They are engaged in a power relationship with their tutors and it may not be in their best interests to voice their negative feelings about them. We all know that students are ready enough to grumble about their course leaders, but it is difficult for them to give sincere, yet critical, feedback directly to them about their teaching. The expression of negative views may be a more reliable source of feedback than the kind of congratulatory comments which tutors prefer to hear. This is not to say that negative comments are necessarily 'true'. Alison may have been wrong in some important sense. So might Andrew. But there can be no denying that their expressions of dissatisfaction must be taken seriously.

Thirdly, students' complaints and difficulties often raise issues concerning professional ethics. Such issues are fundamental to teaching and must therefore be addressed in order to explore the roles and relationships involved in teaching adults.

Teaching is primarily a moral rather than technical activity. Ethical questions must therefore be faced. There will be places in this book where it will be relevant to consider certain techniques for work with adults in some detail. But techniques, or skills, of teaching are always provisional. No technique for working with a student or a group can provide a final answer. All situations are different. The 'constant' of teaching is not the student, or the technique, but the nature of professional judgments we have to make and dilemmas we have to face as teachers.

The nature of these dilemmas and judgments, and the relationships and learning processes in which they emerge, are my subject matter.

The Beginning of an Enquiry

The research for this book took place over six years of working mostly with teachers, but also with other professionals, on a range of courses aimed at developing their practice.

My starting point was a very broad commitment to a student-centred approach to learning gained from my earlier work in schools. At the heart of this approach is the view that, both morally and practically, it is worth taking our students seriously. What they have to say about themselves provides us with the most significant information about their own learning, and thus our teaching. If we can give voice to our students' experience, we have come a long way towards understanding our own practice. Working with adults, it would seem that such an approach was at least as tenable. Since adults are arguably more articulate than children, and are possibly closer to sharing our cultural values, they should provide us with information that is more readily understood.

The opportunity to start this enquiry arose when I was asked to contribute to a full-time Master of Education course being run in my Department. I was to take the sixth of a series of seminars on Methods of Enquiry. The students were mostly qualified teachers working in a range of educational fields. My brief, negotiated with the other tutors, was to encourage them to grapple with a research problem which I had encountered. We would then consider how I had tackled the same problem. This would hopefully lead to a critical discussion of the methods of research in question.

It occurred to me, however, that there was little point in getting the group to respond to a question which I had already answered to my satisfaction, merely as an exercise in research methods. It might be more interesting if they were to tackle an issue concerning adult learning for which I had, as yet, few solutions. Then there would be some chance that I would learn something as well as them. Also, I would then feel that we were 'in it together', which seems to be a good starting point for working with students.

Put briefly, this is the question I wanted them to address. Some years previously I had, as a school teacher, conducted enquiries into learning in school classrooms. Since then I had helped teachers to embark on their own enquiries. But now that I was a tutor of adults on professional courses my teaching, and therefore research, interest primarily related to the seminar or workshop for adults. Could the methods for researching the school classroom be transposed into this adult context?

To help them tackle this, I told them about a brief enquiry I had conducted some years ago in a primary school classroom. This provided a basis for explaining the research and teaching methods which underlay the enquiry. According to this approach, research, conducted by the teacher, is an integral part of the teaching process and should concern itself primarily with the meanings which students give to their experience. Within the context of schools, I have called this kind of research Classroom Enquiry.[1]

The conclusions of this brief enquiry supported two viewpoints: first, that learners are likely to work at a 'higher' conceptual level when they are in control of their learning activity; and second, that it is often inappropriate to pre-determine learning objectives for an individual too narrowly as this may well hold back the development of their understanding.

I was asking my students, then, to consider whether a Classroom Enquiry approach could be used to investigate their own learning and if so, would it be likely to lead to the same kinds of conclusions.

I had already realized that this kind of enquiry would involve becoming more aware of the vastly diverse contexts of thought and feeling which constitute the learning process of professional adults with widely differing experiences. How could this awareness be gained? I had a strong hunch that the students would be able to shed some light on this question. For educational enquiry, as I understand it, is a collaborative process. I felt that what they would have to say would actually matter. After all, it would be their learning which would be enquired into. It would be a matter of engaging them in a research process rather than conducting research on them.

After discussing the background to this question with the students, I left them for a while to talk about it in twos and threes. I suggested that they might consider how they would set about investigating adult learning within the context of their own studies on the Masters course.

Then we reassembled.

My fieldnotes continue the story of this session:

Fieldnote

Once the twelve or so of us were gathered together again, I restated the question:

'Could the methodology of Classroom Enquiry, which we discussed earlier, be used to investigate adult learning on a course such as this? And if so, do you think similar kinds of conclusions might be reached?'

There was a silence. Not too long, but long enough for the group to realize that I was in no hurry to fill it. I had said enough. It was their turn to come up with the goods now.

'The question of how we interact has been totally missed out on this course', said one of them, referring to the Masters course in general. He made little attempt to hide his anger.

'No one has asked us about what we feel about the shape of this course', added another. 'There are no mechanisms for it.'

It soon became apparent that my question had sparked off a torrent of feeling about the course. I didn't want to respond yet. Better to encourage them to say whatever they had to say. I wasn't going to attempt to justify the course structure nor the teaching methods employed by myself and my colleagues on it. Indeed, as a fairly new member of staff, I was quite possibly more ignorant than the students concerning how the other members of staff taught. I was glad they weren't mentioning other tutors by name.

But even so, it was difficult to listen to what appeared to be criticisms of my colleagues without responding in their defence.

'The first thing the lecturing staff need to do is to develop a critique of this course', said one of the group.

How often, I thought, we say this kind of thing to our students, telling them how important it is to develop a critique of their practice. Was the irony intended, I wondered, but said nothing.

His comment led to further criticisms.

'We're not involved enough in the course. We should be able to exercise more control over the activities.'

'The Methods of Enquiry element of the course is irrelevant to the assignment at the end.'

Several nods of agreement.

'The time deadline for the assignment spoils the course. It's just a hoop to jump through and has little to do with my teaching', said a teacher.

I suggested that the group turn their attention to the teaching methods on the course. How did they fit in to what I had said about Classroom Enquiry, with its emphasis upon students controlling their own learning?

'The lecturers try to get away from didactic ways, but the problem is how far they get away from it.'

There then emerged two almost opposite kinds of criticism. According to one, some elements of the course were 'too much like a conversation without any real purpose'. According to the other, the course structure was imposed without any relevance to their needs.

Seeking to clarify this point, I asked the group where they expected this structure to come from. Should it be pre-determined by the course tutor or did they want to create their own structure within each element of the course?

'We need more structure . . . but we would like to negotiate that structure.'

'Yes, more time should be spent negotiating the course structure.'

Several recognized that they would not be in a position to negotiate the structure of an element of the course until they had some idea of the possibilities, that is, the broad field of study.

'I didn't know what I wanted, to start with.'

'We needed some input first.'

By now it was past the scheduled time for the end of the session, and I attempted to sum up what had been said. It appeared that they would like more time to negotiate the structure of the course. They felt that without this negotiative stance on the part of the tutors, there was little chance that we would be able to understand their learning needs. In order to do this, we tutors need to make explicit our own expertise and interests in a general way, and from this point negotiate the structure for the work with the students. The students recognized that this presented problems when they came from such differing professional backgrounds, but there was a general feeling that more attempt could be made to elicit their wishes and feelings. Until some movement was made in this direction, it was difficult to see how access could be gained into the students' thinking, and without this access it would be impossible to conduct an educational enquiry along the lines of the Classroom Enquiry which I had envisaged.

There seemed to be a general agreement with my interpretation of the conversation. I thanked the group for their comments and we departed.

My immediate feeling after this session was that I had not expected a response like this. They had given me few clues as to how I might conduct an enquiry into their learning. No doubt the opportunity which they had grasped to air their feelings was of value to them, and could have provided useful feedback to the course tutors. But it left me feeling somewhat despondent about my investigations. Unless our practice as tutors were to change radically, they were saying, there was little opportunity for me to enquire into the nature of learning on professional courses. Such an enquiry demanded a negotiative approach to learning which, they felt, was lacking.

Upon further reflection, however, I realized that the course participants had in fact told me *exactly* what I wanted to know. For them, the idea of negotiation was central to their learning. Without this they felt merely like rats in the race for the qualification which would be theirs upon successful completion of the course.

A negotiative way of working should therefore be a theme of the enquiry as well as a condition for its success. I would need to understand the processes by which negotiation takes place and how it might affect the tutor's practice and the student's learning.

Understanding this process of negotiation involves exploring perceptions of power and authority between students and tutors and how these are expressed through the dynamics of interaction. It requires a careful questioning of assumptions about personal and public knowledge and how these can be assessed. In the final analysis, it raises questions concerning the aims of professional development itself. But in the immediate term it requires an attempt to reflect upon and make explicit the moment to moment interactions that take place in the seminar room and professional workshop.

The opportunity to consider these questions further arose when I taught on a series of courses for teachers and others involved in education and training. The purpose of these courses was to develop the participants' awareness of teaching and learning processes within their professional contexts. It was natural that, to some extent, they would also want to address questions concerning our own teaching and learning together. Comparing and contrasting our learning together with that in their own institutions would be helpful to them. Such discussions would provide an ongoing evaluation of the course. It had appeared that the students would welcome this kind of involvement, judging by what had been said in the session reported above:

> We're not involved enough in the course. We should be able to exercise more control over the activities . . . more time should be spent negotiating the course structure.

. . . and the implication that lecturers should do more to 'get away from (their) didactic ways'.

This may, however, seem an odd way to work with one's students. After all, they are here to develop their own professional practice, not their tutor's. Or are they? Can we really be teachers, co-learners and researchers together? How clearly do we need to draw the boundary between the tutor and learner within the context of professional learning? These are some of the questions I want to explore in this book.

My expectation is that the planning and reflection of tutors could well be more openly shared with their students. During this enquiry it appeared that such attempts to be open encouraged students to be more forthcoming about their thoughts and feelings. While this is an issue to which I shall return in later chapters, at this stage I chiefly want to emphasize the reciprocal nature of the relationships which I intended to develop with my students who were part of these enquiries. This consisted in a shared concern not only for the subject matter of the courses, but also for the manner in which that subject matter was explored.

In this way the students, whose thoughts, actions and writings will be considered in this book, are collaborators in this research rather than its subjects. If anyone is to be seen as the 'subject' of the enquiry, it is myself, since it is my practice that is revealed and reflected upon here.

Gathering the Material

In this introduction I want to say a little about the kinds of material which arose from this collaborative way of working and which are used to develop and illustrate the lines of argument.

The book is largely concerned with processes of interaction and reflection. Attempting to investigate the quality of such processes amongst a group of people or in a one-to-one tutorial is difficult. Much of what is thought and felt never reaches the surface of speech. As became clear during the enquiry, many of the most powerful experiences arise during moments of silence, or are shared only through the intimacy of private conversation. While public utterances can be recorded and categorized, and even silences can be measured,[2] it is difficult to see how such publicly observable phenomena, analyzed in a quantitative manner, could have shed much light on the nature of thought and feeling as people worked together.

Interviewing participants informally about their experience of group meetings was a strategy which worked at times. But this has its limitations. The first is that it is difficult to recapture the essence of feelings which by their nature are hard to express and are ephemeral. Secondly, such feelings are often personal and revealing of self as well as others in the group, and it may be unwise (as well as unreliable) to expect participants to share them with their tutor after the session. In these enquiries I was concerned to achieve a sense of openness and equality in order that the participants' contributions could be properly valued. This would have been threatened if I, as tutor, were to be perceived as demanding some special access to their thinking and feeling.

The roles of tutor and researcher which, in this enquiry, I was attempting to integrate, are delicately balanced. As a tutor one bears a responsibility for the outcomes of tuition and assessment. As a researcher, on the other hand, one tries to be impartial. While I may often have seen myself as a 'researcher', it was important for me to bear in mind that, for my students, I was invariably their tutor, even when they were talking in confidence to me about their experiences.

Dilemmas such as this are inevitable once one adopts a collaborative orientation towards teaching. They will be addressed at various points in the book.

Fieldnotes made immediately after sessions, often written up in more detail later, are another form of material I have drawn upon. These concerned my perceptions of the events and the thoughts and feelings prompted by them. At times there were opportunities to share these with students so that we could compare our responses. This also provided an opportunity to check up on the accuracy of my recollections.

On some of the courses, students were also encouraged to keep such a log of their reactions and thoughts and these were at times made open to me either in the course of writing formal assignments and evaluations, or less formally. From these reflective writings I often gained an insight into thoughts and feelings which were not hinted at during our sessions together.

Students often reported how, through the process of writing these notes, they were able to recollect and build upon their experience of working together. My approach to this writing was to view it as a serious attempt to portray their own response to the processes involved and not as something to be assessed for its academic merit. But the inevitable student-tutor power relationship imposes limits here as it does with interviewing. While we can aim for a relationship of trust and openness, we cannot expect students to bare their souls to their tutors through their writing.

Such forms of writing as these can give some insight into the experience of learning together, but they can never recapture fully the moment to moment events of group interaction, nor the private feelings which provide its sub-text.

In order to get close to this aspect I have also written fictionally. Fictional writing as a means of exploring professional issues[3] has proved to be useful in a range of contexts. In this enquiry I have used it in two different ways.

First, by fictionalizing accounts, the researcher is able to reconstruct the kinds of events that have taken place in ways which do not compromise the people involved.[4] Such accounts are based upon 'real' events, but their publication avoids questions of confidentiality which would otherwise involve complicated procedures of clearance.[5] Such fictionalized accounts would appear to be common in the writings of therapists and others whose work is of a highly personal nature.

Quite distinct from this is the role of fictional-critical writing (see Winter, 1989). Whereas fictionalized accounts aim to portray an event accurately, merely changing the details from which people might be identified, fictional-critical writing aims to go beyond the 'data'. It aims to open up for exploration the dramatic and metaphysical aspects of experience, rather than to portray real events or provide 'data' from which to construct some kind of universal theory.

Simone de Beauvoir (1946) described such an approach as 'the existentialist way':

> There are two ways of seizing and explaining metaphysical reality. One can attempt to elucidate the universal signification in an abstract language. In this case the theory takes a universal and timeless form. Subjectivity and historicity are utterly excluded. Or one can incorporate into the concrete and dramatic aspect of experience and prose not some sort of abstract truth, but my truth, as I realize it in my own life. This is the existentialist way. And this also explains why existentialism often chooses to express itself through fiction, novel and play (e.g. Marcel, Sartre, Camus). The purpose is to grasp existence in the act itself, in which it fulfills itself. (pp. 159–60)

One does not need to be a writer of Simone de Beauvoir's calibre to recognize the value of fictional-critical writing as a means of investigating the subjective aspects of experience. In this enquiry my own fictional accounts enabled me to 'grasp' some aspects of the processes of interaction which were inaccessible to more empirical methods. My fictional writing about students and tutors was, like any novel, in some sense autobiographical: I found myself identifying both with the tutors and the students I created, but was not committed to a total identification with any of them. It enabled me to imagine myself in roles other than the ones I habitually occupy, and thereby to 'decentre' from my own perspective as tutor.

As the author of such texts, it was important that I should come to view them as a reader, so that I could engage with them critically. It was the meanings in the texts, rather than any supposed intentions which I might have had at the time of writing, which were to be significant. This emphasis upon the reader at the expense of the author (which seems to be particularly vital if fictional writing is to have the critical edge of research) suggests an approach to text like that of Barthes (1977) in which: 'the birth of the reader must be at the cost of the death of the author' (pp. 143–8).

I was helped to view these fictional writings from the position of the reader by sharing them with students or those who had at some point attended my courses. The discussions which followed these readings were crucial in sharpening my own understanding of the issues involved and helping me to view my own texts critically. Where the context for such fictions was the kind of experience which we had shared on a course, people were able to say how they had felt compared to the characters I had portrayed, or how they felt about the tutor I had characterized. On one occasion I was surprised to receive letters from two students with whom I had shared my writings. They had each taken upon themselves the role of a character I had created and wrote to me as if I were one of the other characters.

Such a 'fictional discourse' — a kind of role play — enabled us to confront some aspects of our work together which would have been very painful to have confronted in reality. It thereby became a powerful process in developing the ideas in this book.

I have also made some reference to other writers in related fields of enquiry. The enquiry has taken me into fields as diverse as literary criticism, philosopy, psychotherapy, educational research and social psychology, and it has often been a student who has introduced me to a relevant piece of writing or research. In this way the students' knowledge of other fields, as well as their perspective of the learning and teaching process, has been a powerful source of ideas. There appears to be no one 'field' or 'method' which is appropriate for understanding how we are to learn from each other. My approach is therefore necessarily somewhat eclectic and introspective. It is stimulated more by the kind of reflection which is at the centre of a tutor's professional work, and by the engagement of students with whom an interest was shared, than by a sustained study of research writings and educational theory.

I have used the term 'student centred' as applied to teaching. In the next chapter I shall consider the arguments surrounding this concept in more detail. From this will emerge an approach to student-centred learning in which the roles of tutor and researcher are integrated into one's own practice as an 'enquiring tutor'. It is this approach which underlies the method of enquiry I have used and the rest of the book sets out to explore the possibilities for its practice. Chapter 3 explores a range of dilemmas which inevitably confront the 'enquiring tutor' concerning the relationships between the tutor, students and subject matter.

Chapters 4 and 5 are largely taken up by two case studies which illuminate the experiences of negotiation and reflection which are central themes of the book.

Chapter 6 addresses questions of personal and professional knowledge and how students come to new knowledge. Chapter 7 considers how learning can be evaluated and the role of the tutor and student in this. The final chapter will consider how we can give an account of our professional practice and relate the aims of courses to the development of professional competence.

Notes

1 See Rowland (1984) where this approach is used to investigate the nature of children's learning.
2 Many educational researchers have used methods of categorizing the speech of students and teachers in an attempt to understand methods of teaching and learning. For example Flanders (1970); Galton, Simon and Croll (1980).
3 For a brief discussion of this approach see Rowland, Rowland and Winter (1990) pp. 291–3.
4 This issue is discussed in Walker (1981) pp. 147–65.
5 Questions of the release of data, confidentiality and the openness of research reports have been of particular concern to those involved in action research. The issue is discussed in McKernan (1991).

Chapter 2

An Interpretive Approach to Teaching and Learning

Should the educator take as his model the smith, who roughly pounds the iron and gives it shape and nobility or the vintner who achieves the same result with wine, separating himself from it and shutting it up in the darkness of a cellar? Is it better for the mother to imitate the pelican who plucks out her feathers, stripping herself, to make the nest for her little ones, or the bear, who urges her cubs to climb to the top of the fir tree and then abandons them up there going off without a backward glance? Is quenching a better didactic system than the tempering that follows it? Beware of analogies: for millenia they corrupted medicine and it may be their fault that today's pedagogical systems are so numerous, and after three thousand years' argument we still don't actually know which is the best. (from *The Wrench*, by Primo Levi)

The Background: Pedagogy in Confusion

Educational theories and models, like analogies, should be treated with caution. They are all narratives. They each tell a story, but only one story. They may shed light on an aspect of teaching and learning but, in the process, cast other aspects into the shadows. In a chapter in which I shall present an 'approach' to teaching and learning it is important to be aware of this limitation. It will be no more than a story; but a story which, I hope, will enable me to develop a language with which to explore some crucial dilemmas in working with adult learners. The later chapters in the book will explore these dilemmas. Here I shall begin to construct the story.

For tutors and participants on professional courses, understandings of pedagogy — the relationships between tutor, learner and subject matter — come from a variety of sources. Apart from the broad life experience which we each bring, there is our own experience of schooling, with its wide variety from playing with sieves and yoghurt cartons in the infant classroom's sand tray, to cramming for exams. Then there is the model provided by the traditional university setting with its stereotype of erudite or stumbling professors attempting to introduce their students to the products of scholarship.

From another direction altogether is the rising influence of the 'caring' professions of counselling and therapy with their focus upon the well-being of the subject, variously described as client or patient, with whom a learning relationship is constructed. Theories and practices from this quarter have also influenced training within industrial and management contexts.

Amidst this diversity of experiences upon which to model our own practice as educators, we now also confront an increasing range of government inspired and centrally funded 'initiatives' aimed at helping us to amend our pedagogical ways: Technical and Vocational Initiatives, Youth Training schemes, Training Agency projects, Training and Enterprise Councils, Enterprise in Higher Education, and so on.

Such inititiatives variously speak of 'independent learning', 'student centred learning', 'active learning', 'experiential learning', 'exploratory learning'; terms which have been hijacked from alternative discourses and set to use within the educational establishment whose functions are increasingly ruled by the market. Once it was the mark of a 'radical' to profess the ideals of student-centred learning: part of a liberation philosophy inspired by such writers as Friere (1972) who put forward a project for ordinary people to liberate themselves and transform society by taking control of their learning. Now it is as likely to indicate one's adherence to the popular rhetoric of the educational market place, in which student-centred learning is seen as an effective method for achieving learning outcomes prescribed by higher authority and 'delivered' in the educational market place.

The contradictions are compounded when we consider the urgency with which institutions develop policies of 'equal opportunity' within a social context in which 'free' competition for resources overrides any notion of equality.

Such confusion and contradiction concerning the methods and, more importantly, the values which underly our educational practice, are a feature of our post-modern society. In this climate it is hardly surprising that we become uncertain about our own educational values or, in order to avoid confusion, begin to see our professional practice as primarily a technical activity, and our professional development as no more than a search for the method which works best.

Under these conditions it would therefore seem to be important to try to reconsider some of the fundamental issues and values which, consciously or not, inform our practice as tutors.

Constructing Models

This is the backdrop against which this chapter will consider three approaches, or 'models' which I have found helpful in thinking about my work with adults. In form, the relationship between these 'models' is that of thesis, antithesis and synthesis. In brief, the first model, or thesis, represents the view that the role of the tutor is to impart a body of prescribed professional knowledge (or skill) to the learner. The antithesis to this is the view that the tutor's role is to construct an environmental context in which learners learn as a result of pursuing their own explorations, following their own agendas for learning. The third model is a synthesis of the other two. It views learning as being socially constructed between the learner and tutor with both having a responsibility for seeking to understand each other, as in a conversation.

But first, a cautionary note on the status of the 'models' I shall describe. No real teaching and learning sequence can be described purely in terms of any one of them. They seek rather to provide a conceptual tool by offering three positions against which any real sequence of activity can be compared and contrasted. Like any models, they are also necessarily highly simplified. This is an inevitable consequence of abstraction, which can never take adequate account of the particularities of any real situation. Finally, they are not prescriptive: they do not provide a blueprint for curriculum design. Each does, however, reflect a different value position concerning the nature of knowledge and the roles of tutor and learner in generating and communicating it. My main purpose in presenting these models here is to attempt to clarify these value positions as a basis for exploring how they unfold in practice, and the practical dilemmas which emerge.

The models I shall develop relate to teaching as well as learning, and their relationship to one another in the process of activity and reflection. For this reason, I am not here concerned with how we might learn totally on our own outside any formal or institutional context for learning, except in the sense that we may think of ourselves as having a teaching/learning dialogue with ourselves.

The unit of analysis I shall use is a 'learning sequence'. The time scale for a learning sequence may be anything from a matter of minutes to years. It may be a sequence of conversation during a supervision relating to a problem which has arisen at work; it may be a project which has arisen during a taught course; or a three-year course considered as a whole. It may even be a longer term period of professional development. What unifies the sequence is a common theme which is developed and an ongoing responsibility within a teaching and learning relationship. It follows, then, that small scale learning sequences will be nested within longer term learning sequences.

Two related themes will run throughout these models. The first concerns the control which learners are able to take over their own learning. I mean control here not only over the nature of the learning activity, but also over the conceptual and linguistic features which are developed through the activity. The second concerns the opportunity which the model provides for tutors to enquire into their own practice, for it is the practice of the enquiring tutor which is central to this book.

The Didactic Model

This is the initial thesis: the 'traditional' position in which the tutor has the responsibility of defining the students' needs and providing an appropriate stimulus or instruction for them to act or reflect upon. The students' responsibilities are then to respond appropriately; the tutor's are to evaluate the appropriateness of this response and provide further instruction accordingly. Schematically, it might be represented thus:

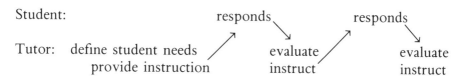

Student: responds   responds

Tutor: define student needs   evaluate   evaluate
          provide instruction   instruct   instruct

In this schema, each new tutorly instruction, is the result of an evaluation of the student response according to pre-specified criteria. As a result of this assessment, the tutor redefines the need and instructs accordingly. The sequence can, in principle, continue indefinitely as the tutor keeps returning to the task of providing more instruction.

To keep things simple, the schema shows an individual student, although there may well be a group or even a lecture hall full of students involved. This also reflects the way in which, in didactic teaching, it is the relationship between tutor and students, rather than between the students, which is considered to be significant.

The first problem which arises for this model is for the tutor to be able to define the needs of, say, a dozen professionally experienced participants on a course. To identify one's own needs is a difficult enough process. To identify those of a group of other people who may be initially unknown would seem to be extremely difficult. For this reason, didactic teaching is the result not so much of an initial *identification* of need as an initial *definition* of need. The sequence of activity is constructed around aims and objectives which the tutor has defined or *pre*-specified as being of value, rather than the result of any investigation to discover what the students think they need.

On the face of it, there are clearly certain teaching methods which appear to conform to this didactic approach. A course of lectures and essays or exams would seem to be a didactic process.

Cantor (1953) described the traditional lecturing approach of universities as being 'symbolic' of a set of assumptions according to which:

* the tutor is responsible for what is to be learned, the student to learn it;
* knowledge, taken on authority, is education in itself;
* education can be obtained through disconnected subjects;
* the subject matter is the same to the tutor as it is to the learner;
* education is primarily a preparation for later life;
* the tutor is responsible for the student's acquiring of knowledge;
* at times students need to be coerced;
* knowledge is more important than the process of learning;
* education is primarily an intellectual process.

These assumptions would seem to be in accordance with the didactic model as I have described it.

It is important to see, however, that other strategies for teaching and learning may be just as didactic. If the lecture is a typically didactic process, a package of programmed learning can often be seen to be even more didactic with its regular sequence of instructions and checks. In this case, the task of instruction may be taken on by the package or textbook but this really only acts as the voice of the tutor. Such a process may achieve the same results as a lecturing format more efficiently, because it allows participants to work at their own speed. But its use may be fundamentally didactic in the way the responsibilities and aims of the educational process are envisaged. Even courses describing themselves as concerned with 'open learning' and 'learning from experience' often fail to challenge these assumptions.

The prominent role of didactic approaches in institutionalized education and training is often viewed as the result of having to work with large numbers of students, or having to meet the demands of public examinations. The difficulty of challenging these assumptions, however, is not only the result of such practical realities.

For example, when I have given a student piano lessons at a mutually convenient time, without any interest in examinations and with no outside pressures, I have still found myself caught in a didactic 'trap'. The student sits down at the piano. I suggest she plays Bach's *Minuette in G.* She plays it. I remark on how she managed the last few bars and suggest she plays them again. She does . . . Immediately we are both caught up in a set of expectations about what it is to teach and to be a student: expectations which are loaded with didactic assumptions. I am the tutor, I know how to play better than her, my task is to tell her what to do so that she will learn what I know. Isn't that what teaching is? To change this process demands that I give a different meaning to my role as tutor. It also demands that I reconsider the nature of knowledge: is it really something I 'have' and can 'pass on'? These are questions to which we must return later.

I hope that from this discussion it is clear that the didactic model (as with the other models which I shall describe) does not describe a *method* but rather a *relationship* and the assumptions held by the learner and tutor which underly it. This relationship may be symbolized by the lecture format in the traditional university setting as Cantor describes it. But more recently it appears to underlie many of the innovations which some have heralded as 'new approaches' to teaching and learning.

As far as control is concerned, in the didactic model control rests with the tutor (or the tutor's materials). The choice of objectives and their evaluation are the tutor's responsibility. It follows from this that the knowledge which results from such a sequence is legitimated by the tutor (or some examination system which, for the learner, represents the tutor). If the tutor is not exactly the source of all relevant knowledge (for example, students may be directed to texts which go beyond the tutor's knowledge), the tutor is the one who decides what knowledge is relevant, what its purposes might be, and whether or not is has been acquired.

With the tutor in such a position of control, this model does not encourage divergent, unusual or individual kinds of thinking on the part of the student. And even any non-conformist ideas that the student may have, are unlikely to be identified by a tutor who is evaluating the students' work only in terms of pre-specified objectives.

Furthermore, it only provides opportunity for the tutor to enquire into the effectiveness of instruction as evidenced by the products of learning and not the processes by which it has taken place, for the tutor has no access to these. For these reasons, it cannot provide a context for an enquiry into the nature of the students' developing understanding and the values by which it is driven.

The criticism of the didactic model as I have presented it rests upon the values and assumptions which underly it, and not upon its effectiveness or its entertainment value (for even lectures can be both effective and entertaining). According to these values, learning is objectively pre-specifiable and measurable and the role of the tutor is to make these pre-specifications and measurements. It exists within a context in which both knowledge and social status are hierarchically determined and serves to replicate these social relations.

It is for this reason that didactic teaching is often seen to be fundamentally anti-democratic and that debates about pedagogy inevitably become political. The rhetoric about education which was reflected in the Black Papers[1] in the late 1960s, and re-emerged in different guises since then, was not really a discussion of method, but an expression of certain political values. In appearing to support a didactic approach against its antithesis, as if this were just a question of teaching 'method', its purpose was to reinforce forms of social organization which are inherently conservative. Thus the didactic model suggests not only a pedagogical programme but also a political one. As a basis for professional education it may be suitable as a means for conditioning adults to professional values as these are understood by the tutor, but in the process will disable them from taking a responsible and self-determining role in the further development of their practice. It is to meet this concern for self-determination in learning that the antithesis of didactic teaching is put forward.

The Exploratory Model

There are a multitude of terms which describe approaches to learning which claim to be totally opposed to didacticism: experiential learning, active learning, independent learning, student-centred learning, open learning are a few of them. Each has been described in many different ways. For example, an international conference on 'Experiential Learning' (reported in Warner Weil and McGill, 1989) defined four different 'villages' or clusters of theorists who have built their ideas of experiential learning around quite different and often conflicting assumptions and concerns. Rather than review these different notions here, I shall propose a model which appears most clearly to provide an antithesis to the didactic model as I have described it.

I shall call this model exploratory, because it is based upon the premise that learning is the result of an exploration of the world rather than the presentation of information about the world. It was most succinctly described by Her Majesty's Inspectors of schools as being an approach in which:

> the broad objectives of the work were discussed with the (students) but then they were put in a position of finding their own solutions. (DES, 1978, para 3)

Applying this model to our context of professional learning, we have a sense here of tutor and participant entering into some kind of negotiation as a result of which the participant embarks upon some item of work or project. This project will throw up problems in its course and the participant will be left to work at these on their own. At the end of the learning sequence or project the tutor evaluates the work. Schematically, this sequence can be represented like this:

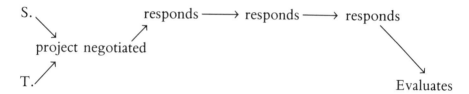

While I have presented this model in a linear fashion, it can, like the didactic model, be viewed as a cyclical process with negotiations for further activity following from the tutor's evaluation.

Here the tutoring role is conceived of quite differently from that of the didactic model. The tutor's task is to provide a rich environment for the exploration and to negotiate activity which arises from that environment. Tutors working in this way may not view themselves as 'teaching' but as helping to organize 'learning situations'. Concerned that learners use their own experience and knowledge to solve their own problems in the light of their own professional values and aspirations, the tutor is careful to maintain a 'neutral' position in regard to values.

In institutionalized educational settings, exploratory approaches have perhaps most successfully been pursued in early childhood education. The idea that young children learn through explorations in their play, more or less structured or negotiated with the teacher, has been common practice in many nursery or infant classrooms in mainstream schools (although many teachers of young children would now argue that developments in the National Curriculum threaten this tradition of primary school practice). The concern for the learner to be free to choose and to pursue their explorations in their own way is central to this approach. In higher and professional educational settings this concern for freedom to choose has expressed itself in new forms. Modular courses at Masters degree level are examples of this, where students are free to choose from a range of optional units which can be put together towards an award. Within any such unit, however, the assumptions which underly the teaching may be exploratory, with students being encouraged to pursue negotiated projects independently. But they may equally be didactic, with little change to the traditional assumptions of higher educational practice.

Like the didactic model, I do not intend the exploratory model to prescribe any particular kind of stimulus from which the learning activity will result. It may emerge from the work place, or a package of distance learning materials, or a role play activity in which a group are involved. The important feature is that whatever the form of the initiating stimulus for exploration, students are free to pursue their exploration in their own way once its overall aims have been negotiated. Only in this way, so proponents of this model would argue, can the students develop their ideas free from the indoctrinating influences that are central to didactic teaching.

Contrary to the didactic model, this approach allows for much greater control on the part of the learners. They are free to use their own experience, their own understandings and their own language to pursue their explorations of issues which they have chosen. The initial negotiations are not intended to constrain this freedom of choice, except perhaps within 'reasonable' limits.

At first sight the exploratory model would also appear to offer greater opportunities for the enquiring tutor to explore the development of students' thinking. For now that they have more control over their activity, and are free to pursue their own ideas, there is a more fertile ground for investigating the development of these ideas.

The model, however, does not provide a role for the tutor within the actual process of the students' learning. In order to preserve their independence from tutorly influence, so that they can solve their own problems, exploration takes place without the tutor. If, during the exploration, the tutor intervenes, this is likely to influence the direction of the work. The assumption of the model is that such influence will pre-empt the opportunity for the students to make their own discoveries.

Aware of this problem, the enquiring tutor might try to intervene gently, in a non dominating manner, in order to try to find out how the student is thinking. The danger here is that the student is likely to interpret this intervention as being some kind of attempt to judge or influence the work, even though this is not intended. Students who are more mature professionals may be more willing to see this kind of intervention as a genuine enquiry on the part of the tutor. But it is surprising the extent to which even the most experienced professional people will be unable to resist seeing the tutor as the expert who is, in some way, intervening in order to redirect or judge the course of activity. Thus, under the influence of the didactic assumptions of the student's past experience of education, the tutor is caught in a 'didactic trap'.

As in the discussion of the didactic model, the exploratory model may be associated with certain 'methods' of teaching, but it is not to be identified with any particular methods. For example, a modular distance learning programme may be didactic, or it may be exploratory; a lecture, too often 'symbolic' of underlying didactic assumptions, may be the initiating stimulus for exploratory learning; even a group seminar may be a genuinely exploratory encounter for the students, without tutorly intervention, or it may be a highly didactic event.

What characterizes a sequence of learning as being exploratory in the terms of this model is the set of values and assumptions which underly it concerning the relationships between tutor, learner and subject matter. In the exploratory model these assumptions centre around a concept of individual freedom: the freedom of the learner to pursue projects which follow their own interests; the freedom of the learner to build their own understandings through their explorations.

A critique of the exploratory model must therefore centre upon a critique of its underlying concept of freedom. This concept of freedom was offered as an antithesis to the domination which the learner suffers at the hands of the tutor in the didactic model. The exploratory model claims to free the student from this.

What the Exploratory Model ignores, however, is that the constraints imposed upon the learner do not only come from the tutor. Our students come from a context which is outside the tutor-learner relationship: the context of their work life, their family and their wider social life, each with its own history. It is these external contexts which, especially for the working adult, may impose a greater influence upon their values than the influence of the tutor. If the tutor is concerned to remain neutral, and to encourage the student to choose their own projects and the ways in which they will be pursued, the result may be that the students' projects come merely to reflect the values of their workplace without any critical engagement with these values.

Let me illustrate this with a case from my own practice. A Masters degree student who was the deputy head of a school was pursuing a dissertation whose aim was to investigate the implementation of the National Curriculum in her school. This was her choice of project and she appeared to have clear ideas about how she was to do this: who she was to interview; the records she would keep over a period of time; and so on. Following our initial negotiations, impressed by her determination and clarity, I encouraged her to pursue the enquiry without further support while she gathered her data and analyzed it. When we met next a few weeks later to consider her work she appeared to be satisfied that she had found out how effectively this new initiative had been introduced to her school.

What she had not done, however, was to offer any critique of the values which underlay this particular Government imposed intitiative. In her place of work, it seemed, there was an overriding acceptance of its inevitability and no-one, including the student, sought to question its values. By reflecting the culture of her own institution, she was unable to provide any critical purchase in her enquiry.

Up to this point in our work, we had operated more or less according to the assumptions of the exploratory model. But to say that this had enabled her to be 'free' is only meaningful in terms of her relationship with me as tutor. She had indeed been free in that respect. But this freedom had allowed her no opportunity to escape from the values which predominated in her work setting. This constituted a lack of freedom on her part.

I am not suggesting that our aim with our students should be for them to embrace values which are hostile to their professional contexts. Nor am I suggesting that our students should come to accept our own values about their professional life. What I am suggesting is that their studies should enable them to question the taken for granted assumptions which may predominate in their work place.

In contrast with the didactic model, the exploratory model rests upon the individual's natural propensity to learn through curiosity and questioning. Such an assumption must surely be valid. It is also a healthy antithesis to the mechanistic notion of learning which underlies didactism. The danger, however, is that it overlooks the wider cultural influences which may inhibit such a questioning approach. In all areas of professional life there will inevitably be factors which inhibit this 'natural curiosity'. An important aim of a professional course must be to counter these constraints upon a questioning attitude.

From this line of argument, then, it would appear that the exploratory model's claim to counter the politically conservative assumptions of the didactic model are limited. It does offer a counter to the authoritarian aspects of the teacher learner relationship, and does recognize the importance of the individual's personal knowledge. In the process, however, it may serve merely to allow students' assumptions to go unchallenged and thereby reinforce taken for granted assumptions about professional life.

Aware of this kind of problem, the tutor is tempted to return to didacticism: 'if students can't get a critical purchase on professional issues by following their own explorations, then we shall have to go back to instructing them'. We are again caught in the 'didactic trap'.

So the didactic and exploratory models appear to exist in a kind of tension. While each is premised upon values which conflict with the other, the tendancy is for the tutor to move back and forth from one to the other. Exploration is encouraged for a period, and then more didactic processes intervene. The danger then is that the student, in the face of this conflict of values, at one moment feels that their own ideas and values can legitimately form the basis of their study, and then at the next feels that they have to conform to the tutor.

I now want to suggest a model for teaching and learning which transcends, or provides a synthesis to, this thesis-antithesis. While it will not provide a solution to all the problems of the previous models it will, I hope, provide a coherent framework from which the dilemmas of the enquiring tutor can be further explored.

The Interpretive Model

The didactic and exploratory models so far discussed share one feature in common. They both appear to view the *learning process* of the student as if it were a black box, a kind of private psychological process in which the tutor cannot engage. The tutor can provide inputs — negotiated or otherwise — and can evaluate its products, but is not involved in the process itself.

In the interpretive model which I shall now describe, this assumption is reversed. Now the tutor attempts to join in the student's reflective processes in order to discover how the student is thinking or feeling and construct shared meanings.

The learning sequence will start with some initiating idea or experience relating to the overall content of the course. This may be offered by the tutor or student, but it is important that, in responding to this, it is the *students'* understanding which predominates. A major role for the tutor is to now engage with students in their process of thinking things through in order to enquire into their knowledge, feelings, values and so on. Through such a process of enquiry, the students come to make their position more articulate, thereby opening it up to question and gaining an understanding of the nature of their problem or interests and what is needed for its solution or development. Once these needs become clear to the student, then they are in a position to delegate to the tutor a responsibility for providing whatever kinds of texts, exercises or instruction may be appropriate in order to meet these needs.

Schematically, the interpretive model may be represented like this:

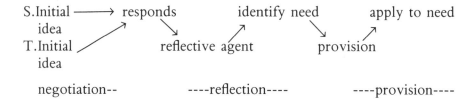

At this stage I have represented the model only in terms of a tutor and one student. I shall later need to expand on this in terms of students who may work as a group, but for now I shall consider only the simpler case of the relationship involving a single student such as might take place in individual supervision or consultancy.

The model suggested three kinds of process: negotiation, reflection and provision. These processes are in no way exclusive since each is likely to play a part in any interaction between tutor and student. The learning sequence does, however, seem to break down into three phases during which each in turn predominates.

The negotiation phase — At the outset of the sequence of learning certain decisions have to be made. Who is going to decide the area for investigation or the subject to be studied? What is its content to be? What procedures or groundrules are going to operate in the tutor and student's work together? These negotiations are aimed towards the student making a response of their own, developing some, albeit tentative, idea of the content area and getting their work 'off the ground'. Their response can be seen as the initial 'action' in an 'action research cycle'.[2] It is important that the student owns this activity and that the tutor is prepared to accept the student's understanding of it.

The reflection phase — Once the student has embarked on some action, enquiry or study, the tutor acts as a reflective agent, aiming to help the student identify concerns and needs, and also to provide positive yet critical feedback to the student. The student, in turn, critically responds to the tutor's contributions. Neither is 'right' or 'wrong'. As Radley (1980) puts it: 'Both student and tutor are engaged in a two way process of expressing what it is they are trying to formulate and grasping those things which the other person is indicating' (p. 42). Bruner (1966) describes the tutor in this capacity as being 'part of the student's internal dialogue' (p. 124).

The contribution of the tutor at this point resembles that of the person-centred counsellor or therapist who tries to approach the student with what Carl Rogers (1977) called 'unconditional positive regard'. It is important, here, to realize that while the tutor's questions may be 'conceived of as ways of getting the students to talk . . . on the whole, it appears that questions may not be a very good means of getting people to talk' (Labov, 1970, p. 29) and that 'there is no way . . . to conclude . . . that the question of one person is functional in another person's thinking (Dillon, 1978, p. 51).

The purpose of the tutor acting as a reflective agent is not to direct the conversation by questioning, but to help the student to make articulate understandings within a supportive context. Working in this way, it is important for the tutor to avoid too anxious a desire to test whether the student's thinking is in line with any presumed training or educational objective, and to have an open mind to the possible meanings of the student's work.

Such a way of interacting with students involves a preparedness to question everyday assumptions concerning the meaning of phenomena: to be open to the strangeness (and indeed ingenuity) of what the students have to say; to be open to what significance they give to their work; to see and listen to them afresh. At times, this means viewing our surroundings as a 'stranger' (Green, 1973): expecting the unexpected and staying with the uncertainties that lie there. It is a perspective which the enquiring tutor, like any fully participant researcher, has to struggle to reclaim as familiarity with the student and surroundings increases (Geertz, 1973).

My description of this process may sound contradictory. On the one hand, it suggests a degree of intimacy and trust between tutor and student which enables the tutor to gain access to the student's emergent thought. On the other, it suggests a distance between them such that the tutor can view what the student says and does without making easy assumptions concerning the meaning of their expression. It is difficult for tutors, with their proper interest in the advancement of their students' professional understanding, and with their increasing knowledge of them, to relate to their students in this way. They need to make a conscious attempt to enable them to articulate their own thoughts. Initially, these are likely to be unclear. But the process of articulating not only reveals, but also develops, those thoughts making them available for critical scrutiny by the student.

The result of this increased clarity and the accompanying critique is often a recognition by the student of needing some new knowledge or skill. Previous assumptions, professional practices or knowledge have been found wanting and now there is an awareness of a lack which needs to be met. At this point the focus of the student-tutor interaction in the sequence of learning changes.

The provision phase — Up till now it has been important for the student to have a controlling influence over the work so that the student's meanings emerge. But now that an awareness has been gained that something else is required, the student is in a position to delegate some responsibility for providing this to the tutor. The tutor's task is now to try to meet this identified need, providing either directly from their own expertise, or indirectly by enabling the student to encounter the expertise of others (other students, external experts, research literature, etc).

From a behavioural point of view, this phase of the learning sequence may resemble the didactic model, with the tutor providing some instruction, or directing the student to a text or task or whatever. But its meaning is quite different. For in this case it is the student, not the tutor, who has identified what is required. The purpose of this provision lies in its application to the student's project or purpose, not the pre-specified objective of the tutor. There is thus, in principle, no question of whether the need is appropriate or relevant: its appropriateness and relevance have been determined by the student. In providing for this need, the tutor is not asserting control as in the didactic model, but providing a service to the student. This process also differs from the didactic one in that the prior phase of reflection has led the student to an awareness of a 'space': a fertile state of mind within which new meanings can grow.

As far as assessment and evaluation are concerned in the interpretive model, both the tutor and the student seem to be in a better position. Through the role of reflective agent the tutor has more intimate access to the process of learning and is therefore better able to provide evaluation of a formative kind concerning the process. As far as the student is concerned evaluations can be made directly in terms of the needs identified and the extent to which they have been met. Such an approach gives the student a much more significant role, particularly in relation to summative evaluation. This has considerable implications for institutionalized assessment, a question which we shall return to in Chapter 7.

As it has been described so far, the model has only related to the individual student. This now needs to be expanded to relate to a group of students who may work with a tutor.

Extending the Interpretive Model

The model as presented could be extended to relate to a group of students merely by replacing the 'student' line of the sequence by 'students'. An important aspect of the model, however, is the relatively equal status it appears to give the tutor in relation to the student. Consequent upon this, the students also, in many respects, are able to take on a tutorly role as they work together in a group. Even without being ascribed formal roles, they will negotiate tasks with each other, act as agents in each other's reflection, and provide each other with new knowledge and skill.

Looked at in this way, the model does not so much describe the relationship between the student and tutor as *people* but the process of learning and teaching in terms of roles. It might well be an aim of a group of people learning together to relate to each other in this way, learning from each other and providing for each other's learning, without the process being formalized. In order to achieve this, the main task of the tutor would be to model the appropriate tutorly role, to establish a culture of educational conversation.

Indeed, an informal conversation between two people can readily be analyzed in terms of the participants severally taking on the different roles represented in the different phases of the model. When the several parties to a conversation behave according to this model, they may initially decide or 'frame' what they are going to talk about (negotiation phase); then share their thoughts, each attempting to understand each other's meanings (reflection phase); then provide new knowledge or perspectives to the discussion (provision phase). A model similar to this is explored by Schon[3] as being a form of interaction which is particularly open to learning.

My purpose in applying this model to conversational analysis is to suggest that the learning sequence itself can be viewed as a conversation, albeit an extended and interrupted one on occasions. Of course many conversations cannot be analyzed in these terms: people don't always help each other to think through their ideas, they don't always try to provide for the needs of each other, and so on. But in principle, the model does suggest a set of values, and identifies some of the features of good conversation. Habermas's concept of the 'ideal speech community' (1974, pp. 32–4), in which participants feel empowered to express themselves freely and to give open criticism to each other in a constructive manner, seems to indicate the ideal of this kind of conversational opportunity.

A limitation of the model might appear to be its linearity. Many theorists portray learning as being cyclical or spiral, such as in the experiential learning cycle (Gibbs, 1988) or the action research cycle. Such models, however, centre upon the process of learning itself rather than the role of a tutor or facilitator in this process as I have attempted to do. In the interpretive model the final stage of the sequence — the application of gained knowledge to the need — might well provide the initiating circumstances for a repeated sequence of learning as the newly acquired knowledge is tested out. This new sequence might involve the tutor again.

From the perspective of the interpretive model, knowledge is viewed as a social construction. While it values the subjective nature of knowledge (as opposed to the objectivist perspective of the didactic model) it is not individualistic (like the exploratory model) instead recognizing the importance of the critical engagement of individuals as they struggle to develop shared meanings.

As far as the learners' control of their own learning is concerned, the model values a sense of equality between tutor and participant before a shared concern for the subject matter. But this is an equality which recognizes the importance of tutors and participants, being mutually critical of each other within a supportive context.

The Role of the Enquiring Tutor

The interpretive model provides a role for the enquiring tutor. The enquiry takes place in the negotiation and reflection phases of the work. It is driven by such questions as: how are the students feeling about this? how does this student understand this? why do these students feel differently from each other? what is the nature of the problem here? (Such questions are quite different from those which drive the evaluations of the didactic model, in which the concern of the tutor is to discover if the objectives have been met.) This enquiry is something the tutor does as a central part of teaching, not as an addition to it.

Research has been described as 'systematic enquiry made public' (Rudduck and Hopkins, 1985). For the enquiring tutor, the enquiry is systematic since it is a central and conscious part of the tutor's way of working. (It may not be systematic in the sense of being codified into a precise set of techniques, for it is not a technical process). It is also made public in that it finds expression and may be opened to critique as part of the ongoing interactions between tutor and learners. In this sense, then, the practice of the enquiring tutor is a research practice. The extent to which this enquiry might be made public to a wider audience, and the reasons for doing so, is something I shall return to in the final chapter of the book.

In this chapter I have provided a rationale for viewing the work of the tutor in professional education as having a form of educational enquiry at its centre. As a pedagogical perspective it appears to overcome some of the difficulties presented by both didactic teaching and its antithesis. The interpretive model attempts to portray the methodology which underlies this research and also to suggest an appropriate relationship between tutors, students engaged in professional learning, and the subject matters in which they collaborate.

It does not, however, provide answers to the moral questions which are central to the practice of teaching in these contexts. Indeed it raises dilemmas which tutors must confront as they attempt to make their role clear to themselves and to those with whom they work. These dilemmas inevitably arise in practice, and it is through practice that I shall attempt to illuminate them in the next chapter.

Notes

1   See especially Cox and Dyson (1969) in which the editors and contributors attempt to defend themselves against the charge of representing a political 'backlash' against 'progressivism'.

2   The following is an example of an action research cycle:

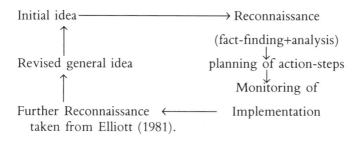

taken from Elliott (1981).

3   See Model II in Chapter 7 of Schon (1983).

Chapter 3

The Dilemmas of Negotiation

There is no means of testing which decision is better, because there is no basis for comparison. We live everything as it comes, without warning, like an actor going on cold. And what can life be worth if the first rehearsal for life is life itself? That is why life is always a sketch. No, 'sketch' is not quite the word, because a sketch is an outline of something, the groundwork for a picture, whereas the sketch that is our life is a sketch for nothing, an outline with no picture. (from *The Unbearable Lightness of Being* by Milan Kundera)

Facing Uncertainty

The tutor's experience of a course lies somewhere between that of the actor 'going on cold' and that of a well scripted event. Planning and past experience can never prepare us like a rehearsal could. Indeed, if it were possible to eliminate uncertainty altogether, we would surely learn little about our students. But if all were confusion, we would be driven mad. Between the two extremes we find ourselves involved in a process of negotiation, as we strive to develop shared meanings, make agreed decisions, come to have expectations of each other, and thereby become a community of learners.

The interpretive model developed in the last chapter identified negotiation as being important, particularly in the early stages of learning together. This is the aspect which I shall explore in this and the next chapter.

The term 'negotiation' carries with it connotations of justice, openness, equality, rational decision making, balancing conflicting needs, and so on. It is hard to be against negotiation. But our work is carried out in a wider social context where justice cannot be assumed, where there is little equality of opportunity or reward, where sectional interests are preserved, where power rather than reason so often prevail, and where past experience of institutionalized education is unlikely to have given negotiation a high priority. In such a context, negotiation is problematic. It involves a struggle as we seek to face the conflicting values within ourselves as well as others. We experience this struggle in the form of dilemmas. What I shall explore here is the nature of these dilemmas as they confront the professional tutor.

But first, I must explain what I mean by 'dilemma' and distinguish it from 'problem'. Problems have solutions which can, in principle, be found, even if we are unable to find them. Dilemmas, on the other hand, have no solutions. The 'horns' of a dilemma represent a fundamental conflict of value or principle. Faced with a dilemma we have to act according to one value or the other, but we cannot act according to both. In deciding which way to act, we have to exercise judgment. Since a principle will be infringed whichever choice we make, the decision has to be made in the light of the particular circumstances.

The argument, which I shall develop throughout this book, is that the professionalism of tutors consists in their ability to confront rather than to suppress these dilemmas. This is a particular case of the more general claim of Schon (1983), that the ability to recognize and face professional dilemmas is fundamental to the concept of professionalism.

Negotiating Contracts

Many writers in the areas of teaching, counselling, therapy and health care have argued for the need to have some kind of contract which provides a basis for the work between practitioner and client. Any course involving a tutor and participants will have an implicit contract, that is, a set of expectations — concerning, for example, attendance at group meetings, or the setting of agendas — which the group implicitly agrees to. It has often been argued that these agreements should be made explicit, thereby forming a recognized set of arrangements which are the groundrules upon which the work of the group will be based. Such contracts, it is argued, are the product of a negotiated agreement by all parties. I want to consider this process of contracting, to see if it provides a rationale for negotiation which is consistent with the interpretive model.

As an example, Egan (1975) argues that to enable adults to learn in an adult way, a contract has to be established in which all group members agree to respect and value each other. He claims that in a contract, formal agreements regarding individual and group boundaries, expectations and commitments along with jointly agreed groundrules of operating, give a much greater degree of freedom to all participants than is possible in groups in which contracts are not established. Amongst a list of things which might be included in such a contract, he includes:

> The kind of influence the helper will exert: 'If I see you trying to avoid doing something that is for your own good, I will challenge you. Or rather I will invite you to challenge yourself. But I will not force you to do anything'. (p. 81)

While such a contract appears on the surface to suggest an open approach to the relationship between tutor and learner (or counsellor and client), only a little analysis suggests that it covers up more than it makes explicit. For example, valuing and respecting persons is not something which can simply be agreed to. People may agree to try to behave *as if* they value and respect one another, but valuing and respecting are sentiments which cannot be legislated for. Nor is the holding of expectations about people. Such objectives may be achieved by a group working together, and they are worth aiming for. But to pretend that they can be agreed to before work starts is to deny the interpersonal effort involved in reaching such objectives. It also encourages a lack of sincerity which is a condition for the kind of relationship implied by the interpretive model.[1]

More dangerously, however, such a contract both hides and reinforces the power of the tutor's role. For it provides an instrument through which any non-conforming behaviour or feelings can be legislated against. At the same time it makes participants feel guilty about, and therefore attempt to suppress, any feelings they have which are contrary to the contract. In this way, the power of the tutor is reinforced by the formal quasi-legislative arrangement, whilst making it appear that it is the contract rather than the tutor which is the source of authority.

In the above example of the kind of thing that might be included in the contract, concerning the kind of influence the helper might exert, we can see this authoritarian streak emerge. Here it is assumed that the practitioner knows what is for the good of the client and should act on this knowledge. Such powerful action is legitimated by the contract. Significantly, Egan does not suggest a further inclusion which would legitimate the client in responding equally critically to the practitioner!

It is difficult to see how the problems of this kind of contract can be avoided as long as it is drawn up by the tutor and then agreement to it is sought from the participants as a condition of the course. Such a procedure is fundamentally technical, that is, it presupposes that the operation of a certain technique (the contract) will ensure effective communication.

If, however, the contract is defined by, and emerges from, the group as a result of a process of open negotiation then, perhaps, the above problems can be overcome. But such a process of negotiation leads to the first dilemma I shall consider.

The Dilemma of Infinite Regress

Working with a group of people on a common task or enquiry, it is a common observation that where no groundrules have been established, certain people are likely to dominate the interaction through the conscious or unconscious use of power, to the detriment of the quality of the group's work. The complete negotiation of groundrules for the group, however, theoretically involves an infinite regress. For, in order to establish what these might be, the group needs to discuss the various possibilities. But this discussion itself requires rules for it to be conducted in a manner such that power is not abused. How are these 'meta' rules to be established, if not by further discussions based upon some yet higher order rules? And so on *ad infinitum*.[2]

This phenomenon often arises in diplomatic negotiations (for example, concerning arms limitations treaties), where 'talks about talks' precede the 'talks', and often things appear to get no further than 'talks about talks about talks'.

So there is a dilemma here for the tutor attempting to negotiate the parameters or groundrules for working together. On one 'horn' the tutor may offer a contract, or some less formal suggestion, concerning the work with little discussion other than an attempt to gain the participants' agreement. In this case it is likely to reinforce, covertly, the tutor's power, as in the example from Egan above. On the other 'horn', the discussion of the contract involves yet further discussions as the group explore the question of how they are going to relate to one another. In this case the danger is that we never get down to the 'real work'.

Such a dilemma cannot be avoided. Rather, professional judgment has to be exercised in the light of the particular circumstances. I shall now give two illustrations of the kinds of judgment which might be made in the face of this dilemma in very different kinds of situation.

Surface Negotiation

The first involved a local government inspector who was running a session for trainee educational consultants. This single one-hour session came in the middle of a longer residential course in which the inspector had not played a part. He comes from a local education authority which places openness and negotiation high on its priorities for management. I was an observer during this session.

Fieldnote

Twenty of us were seated somewhat formally facing the usual overhead projector, screen and flip chart. As he introduced himself, the Inspector, in his dark suit, made a stark contrast with the group of us in our casual dress. He was clearly from 'the office'. In two minutes he outlined the subject matter he was going to address during his talk, concerning the local authority's policies for staff development, indicating that this would conclude with an opportunity to ask questions.

After this brief introduction he looked up from his notes, as if to engage the audience.

'Now that's what I intend to do. But, as you know, in this Authority we believe in the open negotiation of contracts at all levels, so I want to check that this plan is alright with you: that this is what you want me to talk about.'

I was struck by his attempt to appeal to the group here. Did he really want some feedback at this point? What if someone said this wouldn't be a good way to proceed? Would be really leave behind his notes and engage with the group?

The silence following his appeal was a short one. It seemed a mere formality. Apart from a couple of knowing smiles between members of the group who had no doubt heard this kind of thing before, there was no sign that anyone was prepared to suggest an alternative way of spending the next hour.

And so the session proceeded according to plan . . .

The negotiation here is a pretence. The Inspector wants the group to *feel* they 'own' their course, and the part this session was to play in it, and so seeks their consent for what is to take place. He was obviously not expecting to change his plans. No one was fooled into believing that this was a 'real' negotiation, and he would surely have been surprised if the group had openly started to discuss how they would like the session to go. The didactic manner of officials was not really going to change. I felt I had been introduced to the merely rhetorical nature of the authority's claim to emphasise negotiation.

On the other hand I don't think anyone felt they had been cheated. All he was going to do was to make a statement about policy, and everyone there knew that these policies were unlikely to be affected by anything they might have to say. This was really an event for the communication of information, no more. So to have spent time negotiating what was to be communicated and how would just have wasted time. Looked at in this way, the Inspector's 'negotiation' of a contract for the session was a sensible formality: he was telling us what he had to deliver, checking that we knew what the goods were to be, and would then deliver them. It served as an introduction or orientation for what was to come.

Deep Negotiation

My next example takes negotiation to the other extreme. The context for this is a week's residential course, again with a group of teachers about to take on the role of educational consultants in their local schools. As tutor on this course, I had in mind that the detailed agenda for our work would arise from the group concerning the problems they expect to meet as consultants. Soon after the beginning of the course, I prepared the ground for this negotiation by initiating the following 'workshop' activity:

Fieldnote

There were ten of us in the group. Sitting in a circle, I suggested that we give an hour to this activity. At the end of the hour, we could then continue if we felt that would be useful. I described what I had in mind.

The aim was to devise a set of ground rules which would operate during the course. To do this, any participant would suggest a ground rule which could be debated. If all the participants agreed to this rule, it would then be written on a large piece of paper and placed on the floor in the middle of the group. Once a rule was on the floor, everyone had to obey it. They also had a right, and indeed an obligation, to challenge anyone they felt was infringing it. If, at any time, anyone wished to oppose a rule (which they must have agreed to earlier) then the rule was withdrawn or amended in some way. Any rule on the floor had to have the assent of the whole group.

After a few questions in which the rules of this 'game' were checked out, everyone agreed to give it a go.

I was determined to say little once we had started.

Soon John suggested a rule that no one should interrupt while someone else is speaking. Sarah said that this was unnatural: people don't really converse without interruption. This point seemed to be resolved after a little discussion, everyone agreeing that this kind of course was not really 'natural' anyway, and that the rule might help us to listen to one another. John then asked if everyone agreed to the rule. There were nods around the room and so he wrote it down on the floor.

The question of listening to one another was pursued further. How could we make a rule that everyone must listen to what is said? Andy commented that you could not check up that the rule was being obeyed, so you couldn't challenge someone over it, so it wouldn't be a useful rule. Rules had to concern observable behaviour.

Further discussion about this began to get more heated, with John, supported by Jane, arguing for clear-cut formal rules while Sarah protested that such rules were ridiculous if we were really to talk to one another.

Attempting to sum things up so far, Mike said: 'Now where have we got to so far? We've decided that we should always listen to everyone . . .'

'Who's this "we" you're talking about?', interrupted Sarah, angrily. 'Are you saying I've agreed to this? You speak for yourself and let me speak for myself.'

The temperature rose as Jane challenged Sarah for interrupting, then Sarah returned to deal with Mike . . .

. . . The conversation over the next half hour was at times intense, but there were pauses while people gathered their thoughts, or even exchanged the occasional smile. Resulting from the argument between Sarah and Mike, which by now had become more friendly, it was agreed that there should be a rule which entitles people only to speak on their own behalf. After several attempts were made to put such a rule into words, a form was finally settled upon along the lines: 'people must own their own statements and speak for themselves using "I" rather "we"'.

By the time the hour was up, everyone was listening to one another intensely. There seemed to be a sensitivity that was not so much the product of us obeying the rules, but the result of the process of working towards them.

The group felt that the activity was valuable and that we should continue with it in the next session since it had direct relevance to how we interact with colleagues and clients, as well as helping us towards a better way of communicating on the course . . .

In fact, the game was continued for a further two sessions, at the end of which the group decided they no longer needed the ground rules which had been agreed. It seemed that we had come to appreciate the 'spirit' of these rules through the process of progressively clarifying our ideas as we struggled towards an 'ideal speech situation'. In this way, we had come some way towards removing the distorting effects of power on communication.[3]

This example is quite different from the first one. Here I was not offering the content of the course for their agreement (as in the first illustration), nor even offering ground rules for our procedures (as in Egan's contract discussed earlier). I was offering an activity which could have led to the emergence of ground rules, but in fact resulted in an awareness which made such rules unnecessary.

But the dilemma concerning negotiation remained. It was still I who suggested the 'game' in the first place, thereby giving prominence to my own agenda, albeit an agenda concerning process. The negotiation had to start somewhere, and the tutor started it. I could have chosen to refuse to start: to say nothing at all at the beginning of the course and just see what happened. But this itself would have been my choice. A decision not to act is itself an action, a point we shall return to later.

Furthermore, there are questions concerning the power of the tutor in this 'game'. Having decided to join in it, my contributions as tutor were no doubt given a special value. In the fieldnote above, my expressed concern to say little underlines this point. But had I decided not to join in the game, having suggested it, I would have set myself apart from the group and thereby excluded myself from the community which was to be built by its process.

The contexts for this negotiation, and that with the local government inspector, were quite different. One was part of an attempt to communicate information. This required clarity rather than emotional challenge. For the other, which was part of a process of developing the kinds of communication which are important in the role of the consultant, a more challenging climate was appropriate. But in neither case was the dilemma avoided. It could not be.

Most courses have aims somewhere between the two extremes.

Accordingly, the depth or intensity of negotiation might normally lie between the two.

Deception and manipulation occurs when an appearance of negotiation is offered merely to seduce the participants into a sense of ownership of the course without actually empowering them to make strategic decisions concerning the course of events. There is a danger that adopting the rhetoric of the 'negotiated curriculum' can become just such a manipulative device unless we are conscious of the dilemma with which we are inevitably confronted.

The feeling of being manipulated arises when we are aware of a lack of explicitness: when we suspect that we are being driven by a hidden agenda. On courses, we feel, it should be made clear what is expected of the participants and what they can expect to experience. It is possible to do this when the aims of a course are purely technical and predetermined. But when they concern professional or personal values, and are based upon negotiated agendas, there is a limit to the extent to which we can know what is going to happen. In consequence, the activity and its outcomes are bound to be risky.

The Dilemma of Unpredictability and Risk

In the above fieldnote example of the negotiation 'game', it was a straightforward and technical matter for me to explicate the rules. It required no more than clear exposition. The consequences of playing the game, however, were neither simple to explain nor predictable. From past experience, I could judge that such an activity would, in all probability, lead to a situation in which people would directly challenge one another, would be encouraged to take risks, and would at times feel vulnerable. But without prior experience of this kind of activity, the group members were unable to make a very informed judgment about the risks implied by agreeing to work in this way. They were thus put in a position of either taking my suggestion 'on trust' (on what basis could they judge that I was to be trusted?) or merely giving way to my authority as tutor. Furthermore, even if they have experienced this kind of encounter, it will be clear that what takes place is inevitably unpredictable. It will involve some risk, and we cannot know who might be made to feel vulnerable, or might gain insight, or may even suffer as a consequence.

The unpredictability of outcomes is an inevitable consequence of the Interpretive Model's emphasis upon negotiation. This gives rise to a further dilemma facing the enquiring tutor. For what right has the tutor to subject students to risk?

There seem to be two different kinds of risk involved in learning. One is the risk that our students will not learn what they are supposed to. The other is that learning involves the risk of discomfort or even pain as participants engage with one another and their familiar understandings are challenged.

Concerning the first kind of risk, it is important to emphasize that any kind of teaching is highly unpredictable in its outcomes. Even the most structured lecture cannot come with a guarantee that its objectives for the students' learning will be met. Where learning in the short term does seem fairly likely — as, for example in the rote learning of a procedure — there is very little certainty that the learning will be retained and even less that it will be transferable to other situations.

Current concerns to identify precisely the training objectives of courses are an attempt to avoid this contradiction between the unpredictability of learning, on the one hand, and the attempt to pre-scribe its outcomes, on the other. For example, recent developments in research training in higher education contain such 'targets' as learning the 'skills' of enquiry methods. But clearly, people can only be taught how to enquire by enquiring into something. But of its nature, enquiry is unpredictable. Its success cannot be guaranteed. Enquiry often leads to dead-ends, to failure and frustration as well as to discovery. In order to 'teach' such aspects of a course the participants must be given a large degree of control of the learning situation — as indicated by the inter-pretive model, for example — for otherwise the process would not be one of enquiry. But if they are given this degree of control, then we can never be sure of the learning which will result.

So we arrive at the dilemma that in order to teach such things as enquiry methods, we have to teach in a manner which cannot ensure that such aims are achieved. In other words, effective tutors can never be sure that their teaching is effective! This paradox is born out by experience, for the most enlightened tutors often feel doubts and uncertainties about their ability. Indeed pedagogy, it has been argued, *is* this questioning, this doubting.[4] Such creative self-doubt is funda-mental to any artistic, rather than technical, endeavour.

The same argument applies whether we are considering teaching enquiry methods, or the ability to counsel, or to develop management skills, or indeed many other of the abilities which are the concern of the professional person. The learning outcomes of any course which deals with such things are necessarily unpredictable. The approach suggested by the interpretive model cannot therefore be ruled out on the grounds of the unpredictability of its outcomes alone.

There is, however, another kind of risk involved in the negotiative aspects of the interpretive model which presents more of a problem. This is the risk of discomfort or pain associated with the unpredictable (rather than simply tedious or strenuous) nature of the learning process.

Counsellors, therapists and religious prophets often speak of the pain associated with personal change or learning. They often emphasize this aspect, rather than the joy which also accompanies learning. But it is the possibility of pain which gives rise to a moral dilemma. For the interpretive model, with its emphasis upon learners' control and therefore responsibility for their own learning, the dilemma is particularly acute. Can it really be right to place our students in a situation which they may find painful, in ways which we cannot predict, and for the sake of an educational or professional outcome which remains uncertain, and then hold them responsible for any pain which they might experience?

Therapists attempt to overcome this moral dilemma in various ways (although some would argue that it is not adequately acknowledged).[5] Their clients usually come voluntarily without pressure being exerted by professional institutions; they usually have some idea of what to expect; sessions are strictly timed and scheduled so as to reduce anxiety; therapists have supervisors with whom they can explore their own anxieties which arise from the process; and the client-therapist relationship is normally held within tight professional bounds. Freud even went to the lengths of placing his clients on a couch in such a way that eye to eye contact was not possible. Such strategies no doubt insulate the therapist from sharing the pain of the client, but not from responsibility for it. Fritz Perls is a Gestalt therapist whose work addresses some of the issues of learning which are of concern to us, especially the idea of learning from experience. In his view:

> Learning is discovery. There is no other means of effective learning. You can tell the child a thousand times 'The stove is hot.' It doesn't help. The child has to discover it for himself (sic). And I hope I can assist you in learning, in discovering something about yourself. (1969)

In the taped transcripts of his own workshops it appears that in order to help his (adult) clients to 'discover something' he not only assists them to touch 'the stove' but indeed pushes them onto it. Within five minutes of working with Fritz, his client is usually experiencing some kind of emotional pain. It is difficult to see how he can avoid responsibility for this.

In educational and training (as opposed to therapeutic) institutions we are unaccustomed to viewing learning as being painful in this way. While academic learning and training may be boring, tedious or frustrating, it is not usually seen as being painful in the way that a therapeutic experience may be. Academic learning and training are often viewed as being different from personal learning as if the head and the person were two separate organs, or as if the 'professional' and the 'person' were two separate beings. The very term personal skills (and even transferable personal skills) so prominent in current courses designed for the 'helping professions', seems to imply that the rest of professional education is not personal, or that 'personal' can be distinguished from 'intellectual' learning.

We recognize the personal dimension of learning through our concern to place learners in a position where they have more control over their activity. The 'curriculum' ceases to be a body of knowledge and skill which exists outside them and independently of them, but becomes part of the meaning which they give to their life experience. In this way, the interpretive model is holistic, involving all aspects of the self, not just the intellect. Thus the risks involved are not only those of mental effort but also of emotional disturbance.

This makes the dilemma for the enquiring tutor more acute. It is one thing to place one's students in a situation where they risk the pain of mental effort, quite another if the risk concerns their emotional well-being. But if professional learning is more than merely the acquisition of technique, and it is to take place in a context of negotiation, then there will inevitably be some element of risk.

Dilemmas in Providing Structure

With some awareness of this dilemma, some researchers have argued that the most effective climate is somewhere between one which generates too much 'success' (associated with lack of risk) and one which generates too much 'stress' (associated with risk) (see, for example, Roskin, 1976). Exactly what constitutes 'effectiveness' and 'success' for these writers seems problematic, and is something which will need exploration in a later chapter. The point at issue here, however, is that there is, perhaps, some middle ground which provides enough risk for valuable learning but not so much as to place the participants (or tutor) under too much stress. On the face of it, this would seem to be a plausible idea.

The problem with establishing this middle ground between 'success' and 'stress', however, is that any situation will provoke a different degree of stress in different individuals. Some find it stressful to express their feelings openly; others are intimidated by intellectual demands; some enjoy confrontation; others shy away from it. In general, the uncertainties associated with a negotiated approach to learning may provide a sense of adventure for some students; for others they may place at risk the security they need if they are to contribute fully.

The unpreparedness to cope with uncertainty is often experienced as a need for structure. Some participants appear to require a good deal of structure, others to need little. It has been suggested that:

> Individuals with highly programmed jobs and individuals who have experienced or are experiencing a highly programmed education may have learned to require a high degree of structure, regardless of the kind. On the other hand, individuals who are accustomed to operating autonomously and who have more self-directed learning experiences, may learn best and be most comfortable in formats with less structure. (Walter and Marks, 1981)

In a situation where little direction is given, those who require more structure are likely to latch on to almost any intervention on the part of the tutor as a directive or an opportunity to provide structure. This can make it impossible for the tutor to intervene as a co-learner for, upon any attempt to do so, she or he is forced back into the traditional 'leadership' role.

On the other hand, if the tutor does not intervene, this is likely to appear to be manipulative, since the tutor is deliberately withholding knowledge and experience. Such a course of action (or non-action) contravenes an implicit norm of the group for openness, while at the same time may make participants feel that there is a hidden agenda which is not being shared with the group.

Individual Differences

It may seem that a concern for open negotiation should lead to open structuring, for it works against the tutor imposing directions upon the group. Paradoxically, however, if the tutor is really concerned for the group to devise its own structures for work, this can have quite the opposite effect. Given this freedom from the tutor's direction, those individuals who require a high degree of structure will often exert more influence than those who require little.[6] In this way tight plans and procedures can emerge from the participants against the interests of those individuals who want more openness. Such a process will move the activity away from the interpretive model, if the negotiation results in sequences of activities which are pre-planned with little room for reflection and redefining needs.

This appeared to be the case during a course in which I was a participant observer, working alongside a colleague. In this instance, the tutor was concerned that the students should plan their own programme for a short course. The result was a detailed programme, constructed by the group at the beginning of the course, in which all the time was to be taken up with planned tasks. Reflecting on this course later, Suzanne, one of the participants, wrote a poem which expressed, among other things, her frustration about the pre-planned nature of the activity. This extract from her poem takes off from the point when the group was settling down around their word processors to the second day's work of the programme:

In Room 6 at nine thirty the next day
Monitor, as power is established,
With buffer zones and interface set up.
Time to begin — Everything accomplished,
However, overloaded circuits lack
Operational ability and we are pitched into the black.
For suddenly . . .
'Not now!
This is not what I need!
I don't want to do this!'

But that's the plan.
You have to stick to the plan
You can't change the plan.
We all agreed to the plan.
We have to follow the plan.
For we are grown-up and we can cope when we have a plan.

And later in her writing, she refers to her attempt to move the group away from the agreed plan and onto more open-ended activity:

. . . I question what people want from this course.
There's a unique opportunity here
To be different, to investigate
The unknown. But there is a growing fear —
An awareness that we are loosening

> The thongs from the plan's own straight-jacketing.
> And as a grown-up, we do not know if we can cope.
>
> Trampling well-worn paths, never digressing.
> Route-weary destinations to depress.
> Divert, explore the thorny areas.
> Climb the boulders, allow life to express
> Itself. Discover places of beauty
> And relax, content, at peace. Unity.
> For you are a grown-up and you can learn to cope.

Suzanne's attempts to try to pursuade the group to work in a more exploratory way involved her taking enormous risks which were painful for her as she was seen by others to be going against the 'contract', to which she had been a party, concerning the planned programme. The experience led her to write twenty-four stanzas each ending with a refrain about being 'grown-up now' and able to 'cope', expressing her awareness of the difficulties of coping with the difference between her own needs for openness and those of the group for a tighter structure. The difficulty for her would have been avoided had the participants been able, at various points, to alter their involvement in the light of what had already happened and their anticipation of what might happen next.[7]

These differences between the needs of individuals present a dilemma which is likely to be experienced, amongst any group of people who negotiate their work together, as they struggle to balance their own needs with those of the group.

Working in groups, however, it is important not to reify the group: to conceive of it as a being, with a will of its own distinct from those of its members. This tendency to give 'the group' an overbearing authority can be disempowering for the individuals in it as they each suppress their individual needs to the perceived, and somewhat mythical, needs of the group. Certain brainwashing techniques, and even the T-groups so popular in the 60s, have been criticized on these grounds (see, for example, Harvey, 1971, pp. 33–5).

Theoretically, rational debate, conducted within an 'ideal speech situation', will lead to consensus.[8] It does not follow, however, that the aim of reaching consensus ensures the emergence of an 'ideal speech situation'. On the contrary, the distorting influences of power within a group may well be exacerbated by a premature concern to reach consensus and a misplaced belief that this is in the interests of the group.

Nevertheless, group norms will inevitably emerge as individuals work together. At times individuals are bound to experience a conflict between their own requirements and these norms, or between their own needs and what they perceive to be the needs of the group. In the above example of Suzanne's poem, we saw how she had to struggle with this conflict. In this next example, another student, Theresa, reports how the group with whom she was working came to terms with their differences:

> The growing sense of closeness that developed in the group did not depend on a resolution of the conflict of opinion and personality that emerged, but on the acceptance of our differences. Just as we were able to accept that people could withdraw from activities and did not become less part of the group by doing so, we were also able to accept that having different opinions did not affect our positions in the group. Indeed, it would be hard to say that at any time there was a 'group opinion' from which others could differ; we were experiencing something to which we all brought our differences . . .
>
> . . . I remember listening to someone speak and experiencing something like a shock of recognition. Every word confirmed their 'not-like-me' ness, the differences in the way we thought and the things we thought about, and I was not simply accepting those differences but delighting in them. I began to think about other people not like me, in a new way.

It is interesting to compare this 'delight' in differences with the Rogerian notion of acceptance and 'unconditional positive regard' which was discussed in the last chapter in relation to the reflective agent role within the interpretive model. While the Rogerian notion seems to cast the practitioner role in a somewhat detached relation to the client role, Theresa's 'delight' indicates a more lively positive engagement from which the participants were able to act as reflective agents to each other. Her description of the 'closeness' of the group suggests that 'the group' was a strong construct for her, but it was one which celebrated rather than suppressed individual difference.

Needs Clarification

The further we go down the path of negotiation, the more the differing needs and values of the participants are brought to the surface. While this can lead to conflict between individuals which are real enough, it can also lead to fragmentation amongst the group as people begin to identify with certain positions which they presume to be shared amongst sub-groupings. The group can then become locked into a situation where it is impossible to make decisions or reach consensus. In this next extract from my fieldnotes I describe an attempt to unlock such a situation:

Fieldnote

The group of eight of us had by now, been working together for about eight hours in all. A number of activities had taken place and between these there had been several discussions about how the programme of work should develop. It seemed to me that there had now emerged a difference amongst the group, as if we were two 'camps', who wanted to do different kinds of things.

As we tried to decide on the next activity, it seemed that we were having problems coming to any decisions. The discussions were going round in circles and people were getting a bit irritated with each other. I felt there was a lack of clarity. It seemed fair enough to expect that we have different needs, and wanted to do different things to meet those needs, but until we could become a little clearer about what those needs were, I didn't see how we could make any useful decisions. In the meantime the atmosphere was becoming increasingly uncomfortable and I wondered whether we were really listening to each other. Perhaps we were each trying to promote our own interest and therefore getting nowhere as a group.

It occurred to me to make a suggestion to try to get us over this problem. After giving the matter a little thought this is what I suggested to the group.

I offered to structure a session whose purpose would be to clarify our needs.

The group seemed happy to listen to my idea, so I continued.

Sitting in a circle, we could take it in turns to be 'it'. When someone was 'it', then each member of the group would say, in turn and without any discussion, what they thought the 'it' person wanted from the group, or wanted to do or to talk about. We would go round in the circle each saying what we thought about the 'it' person in these terms. Then, when everyone else had spoken, the 'it' person should respond to what had been said about them, saying what they felt was correct about themselves, and correcting any misconceptions people had about their needs.

I suggested that if we did this, with everyone taking it in turns to be the 'it' person, then perhaps we would have a clearer basis for making any further decisions.

The group readily agreed to this suggestion.

(Were they agreeing, I wondered, because I was the 'tutor'? Would they have so readily agreed if the decision had come from someone else, given the amount of disagreement there had been so far? Was this kind of intervention one which would simply encourage the group to look to me to solve its problems rather than work through them together? These were some of the uncertainties in my mind as I made my suggestion.)

They decided to choose who would start off being 'it' by spinning a bottle in the circle and seeing who it would point at when it came to rest.

I don't want to go into the details of what was said during this clarification exercise. Rather, I want to consider some of the conclusions we came to.

The most remarkable effects of the exercise were realized during further discussions afterwards. It became very clear that it had got us to start listening to each other much more carefully. It seemed that it had, in a way, legitimated the positions that each of us held. Now that the differences between participants had been acknowledged, it appeared that there were no longer two 'camps' in conflict, but rather a wider spread of interests. From this realization, it was not only easier for individuals to recognise the need for some degree of compromise but, more importantly, there seemed to be a growing ability to value the different perspectives being offered. We were therefore more able to accommodate to each other and work more collaboratively.

Something else that really struck me was how accurately we each perceived each other. In spite of all the earlier difficulties in communication it seemed that we did, in fact, have a very clear idea about each other and what we each wanted. The occasions when the 'it' person in the concluding talk-back rejected something that was said about them was the exception. We all felt supported by the experience of being given the attention of each person in the group, and then finding that everyone had such a good idea of what we wanted.

What is interesting in this example is that while there was initially a strong perception of two 'camps', once we had actually brought our judgment to bear on each individual, this perception largely dissolved.

From then on negotiation could continue without the need to defend the supposed 'camps', with the inevitable distortion in communication which accompanies such a 'power struggle'.

The discussion of individual differences has so far related to the participants rather than the tutor specifically. The tutor, however, has a perspective which arises from tutorial responsibilities and an interest in enquiring into the nature of the course itself. This gives rise to a particular dilemma for the enquiring tutor.

The Dilemma of the Tutor's Enquiry

This dilemma relates to our central question: How can tutors be both researchers into their own practice and tutors at the same time? While I present the case in this book for research into the practice of tutoring being a fundamental aspect of the role of the professional tutor, there will be times when the teaching and research roles come into conflict.

This dilemma is faced by any professional who has a responsibility for both serving the needs of other people and, at the same time, exploring and developing new ways of doing this. Consider, for example, the medical profession. Here there is a responsibility, enshrined in the Hypocratic Oath, to give priority to the needs of the individual patient. In prescribing new treatments, however, the doctor may also have a research interest: to investigate the effectiveness of a new drug by making various measurements, comparing its effectiveness against that of 'control groups', and assessing the course of treatment in other ways. While such research will be in the service of patients in general, it may not serve the interests of the particular patients involved in the trials.

But medical treatments, and research into their use, are primarily seen as technical processes for which experimentalism may be an appropriate basis for conducting research into their effectiveness. In medicine it is therefore generally (although not exclusively) a technical matter to build safeguards which protect the individual patient so that they are not unwittingly used as 'guinea pigs' in research experiments.

Unlike the medic, the enquiring tutors' practices are not 'treatments' which can be tested in advance. Every encounter with a student provides, to some extent, a 'field' for the tutor's investigation. In this 'field' the tutor has an interest — to discover things about teaching and learning — an interest which is not necessarily shared by the student. This enquiry interest will place demands upon the tutor's resources of time and energy, resources which might otherwise be more directly related to the students' needs. What happens when the tutor's need to enquire comes into conflict with the students' interests? Should the tutor's needs always be subordinated? It may be in the interests of our students in general that we approach our work with them with the interests of our enquiry given prominence — for that is how we learn and become better practitioners — but is it always in the interests of these *particular* students? Can we be sure that we are not using them as 'guinea pigs' in our own search for understanding?

These kinds of questions were of particular concern for me on a series of optional courses I ran for people from a range of professions. The aim of these courses was to explore the issue of how, as a group, we could negotiate our own learning activity at the deepest level, that is, without accepting any assumptions about who should facilitate the process of negotiation. While it was hoped that these courses would be of value to those who participated, they clearly had a research interest for me as a way of exploring the kinds of issues dealt with in this chapter.

I came to wonder, however, whether these courses were aimed to meet my needs for learning rather than the students'. As I began to give more time to reflecting upon every detail of the developing dynamics of the group, was I adequately responding to what the participants wanted from me?

Ivy, a student on one of these courses, chose to write about her experience through a fictional dialogue in which the two characters talking represent two opposed parts of herself as she struggled to make sense of dilemmas which it had raised for her. In this somewhat ironic interchange concerning my role as the tutor, one of the characters suggests that I am pursuing my own research needs rather than the students':

Seems to me he gets the best of all worlds: no lectures to pre-pare, transfer of responsibility to the students and a chance to watch a group in action. I bet he uses the material to write his research papers as well!

Yes, I think he does, but that isn't necessarily wrong — it's a question of motivation. I think he is genuinely interested in the issues of active learning — and far from skiving off work it takes a lot more strength and security to start out on a course where you don't know what's going to happen than to work methodically through a prepared set of lectures.

It was some consolation that at least one of Ivy's characters considered that my 'genuine interest' was appropriate in this case. Significantly, she makes this judgment on the basis that I am motivated by the same concern as the students: a concern to explore the nature of what she called 'active learning'. But I am nevertheless confronted with the possibility that as long as a course is an exploration (which it should be), it may be one which meets my needs as an explorer rather than my students'. This was the position adopted by the other of Ivy's characters, who implies that the students' interests may have been subordinated to my research interests. Through the two characters Ivy had identified the dilemma in which I found myself. She had written these thoughts as a dialogue because she was unsure about which 'horn' of the dilemma she sided with. Neither could I dispel my doubt.

Viewing the students as collaborators in the research of the enquiring tutor has been my intention in this book, and in the research by which it is informed. Inasmuch as I have achieved this in practice, and the research interest has been a shared one, I have avoided the dilemma. In most work with students, however, tutors cannot assume that their research interest in the processes of their work together will be shared by their students. To that extent it seems important that the tutor's concern for enquiry does not override an awareness of the students' needs of the moment. Without that awareness, our research may lead to psychological knowledge, but it will not be educational.

Freud proposed the term 'epistemophilia', whose etymology suggests the meaning 'the love of knowledge', which he places beside the desire for sex, money, domination, power, submission and many others.[9] It is interesting to contrast this word with 'philosophy' — 'the love of wisdom'. Perhaps the enquiring tutor needs to be a practical philosopher without being an overbearing epistemophiliac: to temper a desire for knowledge with a wisdom which takes into account the part which ethical and educational values play in the transactions between learners and teachers.

In this chapter I have outlined some of the dilemmas that arise in the attempt to follow the interpretive model's emphasis on negotiation. I have suggested that in facing these dilemmas there are no clear prescriptions or techniques which can be generally applied, and that each situation has to be faced in the light of the particular circumstances. In the next two chapters, which concern the movement between the negotiation and reflection aspects of the interpretive model, I shall focus in much more detail on the particular. In this way I hope to bring to life the work of a group as it prepares itself for new professional knowledge.

Notes

1 This is a relationship in which participants strive towards what Habermas calls an 'ideal speech situation', one condition for which is sincerity. See Gibson (1986).

2 'Ground rules' here constitute a particular educational theory. As Wilf Carr argues, educational practice cannot be totally determined by educational theory since the choice of any such theory would have to result from the application of a meta-theory, and so on. See Carr (1987) pp. 163–75.

3 For an interesting theoretical discussion of the search for successful communication, with reference to the work of Habermas and Godamer, see Thompson and Helds (1982) chapter 6, pp. 116–33.

4 For an interesting paper on pedagogy as questioning and doubting, see Van Manen (1989) pp. 437–52.

5 The case against therapists in this regard is forcefully presented in Masson (1989).

6 This feature of a group's dynamic is discussed more fully in Bormann (1990) chapter 4, pp. 76–100.

7 This is a strategy suggested in Kelman (1965) pp. 31–46.

8 This is discussed in relation to Habermas's theory in Thompson and Held (1982) pp. 42–56.

9 For a discussion of the relationship between critical theory and desire see Gibson (1986) chapter 6, pp. 118–39.

Confronting the Unknown:
A Case Study

In order to arrive at what you do not know
you must go by a way which is the way of ignorance.
In order to possess what you do not possess
you must go by the way of dispossession.

(T.S. Eliot, *East Coker*, 138–141)

Introduction

This chapter takes the form of a detailed case study of a short course which set out to explore what happens when a group of people negotiate their own learning activity together, without any prespecified content. It aims to bring to life some of the dilemmas explored in the previous chapter and portray how a group of students responded to them.

The participants were all involved in some form of teaching, training or therapy and took the course as an optional unit on a Master in Education programme. The course was titled Active Learning because this is a term which highlights notions of ownership and negotiation and has increasing currency among teachers and trainers.

While there appear to be no clear definitions of active learning, most discussions of it centre around such claims as: learning is based in direct experience; learners are, or should be, responsible for their own learning; they have, or should have, the right to exercise a degree of control over what and how they learn. If such conditions are to be met by a group of people working together, then negotiation must be central to the process of their work. These were the kinds of things which we sought to explore on this course through the process of our own negotiations and learning together.

The chapter is in two parts. Part I is an account of the course from my own viewpoint as its tutor, drawing upon some of the themes identified in the last chapter. Against its backdrop, part II presents selections from the writings in which the participants reflected on their experience of the course. In this way I hope to provide a multiperspective account of an exploration in negotiation in order to illuminate the issues raised by the negotiative aspects of the interpretive model.

Part I: The Course

Preparing for the Course

A brief paragraph in the MEd brochure described the course as being 'experiential', as aiming to develop some of the central issues of active learning, and as involving a high level of student participation. It was to consist of two introductory evening sessions, a weekend residential workshop (Friday evening until Sunday midday) and two follow-up evening sessions.

I wrote to those who applied for a place on the course five months before the residential weekend. My letter gave the dates of the sessions and made clear that it was essential for all participants to attend all of them. It also advised that participants may submit work resulting from the course for assessment as part of the Masters' programme or, alternatively, may prefer not to submit work. I also offered to make myself available for further tutorial support after the sequence of formal sessions for those who wished.

Together with this letter I sent some very brief notes which suggested that some of the dilemmas and confusions which are discussed in the previous chapter might be involved in active learning.

Before the group met at the first introductory session, however, I also had in mind certain parameters within which I saw the course operating.

Being experiential, I envisaged that the course would focus upon our own learning, rather than learning in classrooms, counselling sessions or other professional contexts. If we could gain some understanding of our own learning 'here and now' on this course, then, perhaps, we would be in a position to explore how such understanding might influence our work elsewhere.

I had in mind that the course should aim to test the rhetoric of active learning. By this, I meant that the claims concerning student responsibility and the negotiation of activity were to be taken literally.

This was to be a genuine exploration since, taking these claims seriously, I had no way of knowing what the content of the activity would be. Furthermore, upholding the principle of equal responsibility, there was no reason why I, rather than anyone else, should take on a facilitator role in the process of negotiating what we were to do. I was therefore, in a sense, abdicating my role as tutor of the course by suggesting that I saw myself as having no particular responsibility, accept as an equal participant, for the content of the course or the process by which we would work together.

I realized before the first session that I was placing myself in a contradictory situation. This was a university course for which the students (or their sponsors) paid a fee; I was employed to run it; I would (in all probability) be asked to judge any work submitted for credit; I had brought the group together; I would reasonably be expected to have more experience in this kind of work than most of the participants. For these reasons, whether I liked it or not, I was the tutor and was not in a position to claim that I wasn't. If I chose not to exercise my responsibility with regard to the content and process of the course, that was a choice I was making as tutor. Paradoxically, my deciding not to facilitate the process was, itself, the way in which I chose to facilitate it.

I was also aware that such a non-directive approach is open to the charge of being manipulative. For since I, in reality, had overall responsibility for the course, wasn't any attempt to abdicate this merely a pretense? Wouldn't I merely be attempting to delude the participants into thinking that we shared responsibility in order to perform a social or educational 'experiment' at their expense, and with possible risks which I could not foresee?

These problems caused me considerable anxiety before the course started, and at times emerged to haunt me during the course. In an attempt to confront them, I made two resolutions before the first introductory session.

First, I would attempt to be open at all times during the course to sharing my own anxieties, and attempt to make explicit any agenda I had. While I did not wish to impose the problems that my own contradictory role made for me, upon the group, it was important that I should be open about them, just as I hoped that the other participants would be open about their problems. I reasoned that just as my role as a 'tutor' in active learning now presented me with dilemmas, the other participants would, if they were to use active learning principles in their own work, find themselves beset with similar dilemmas.

Secondly, I would limit the extent of my abdication from the course tutor role. I would manage all the administrative arrangements for the course. During the introductory sessions, although I would attempt to encourage full participation, I would facilitate the process so that, with luck, we would approach the weekend with some shared understanding about its purpose. During the residential weekend itself I would try to work as an equal member of the group rather than as a facilitator. During the follow-up sessions and any informal tutorials I would, if the group wanted this, provide whatever support they felt they needed in order to produce some product for assessment. I hoped that by putting these limits on the 'leaderless' aspects of the course, everyone would be happy to approach the weekend without too much anxiety.

With these feelings and resolves I approached the first introductory session.

First Introductory Session: 13 March 7.30–8.30pm

Ten of us were present. An ideal number, I thought. After each introducing ourselves briefly, I suggested that people talk to the person sitting next to them for about ten minutes in order to share their feelings about the course, what they expected from it, any hopes or fears they might have, and so on. This led naturally to a full group discussion during which time I also attempted to make clear the purpose of the course as I understood it.

As I had expected, a major concern in this discussion was the lack of planned activity for the course. Some people seemed anxious about this. 'How will I know this is going to be worthwhile unless I have some idea about what we're going to do?' perhaps typified their feelings. Others felt differently. For them, the lack of a plan was exciting, or challenging. As the session progressed the participants seemed more and more to divide into two similar sized groups: those who welcomed the lack of a plan, and those who felt anxious or even hostile about the uncertainties involved.

Another issue which emerged much more strongly than I had anticipated concerned the possible painfulness of the experience. Two or three people who had prior experience of working in a counselling or therapeutic framework, or who had heard about a course I had run the previous year, expected that such a course without an agenda or established procedures, was likely to be difficult or even painful at times. It was suggested that people might be hurt during the experience, that some kind of support was needed, and that we needed to address this issue straight away. The problem was raised not as an argument for a clearer structure, but as a precaution we should take.

It seemed to me that those who had already expressed their qualms about not having plans were now made even more anxious by this talk of pain. What was going to be painful? Active learning should be fun not painful. Did someone know that something dreadful was likely to happen, but wasn't letting on? What was this all about?

I felt pressure upon me to provide an explanation. But that was not easy. The allotted time for the end of the session was approaching and some people had other engagements to meet. I didn't feel that whatever I said was very helpful, and drew the meeting to a close suggesting that people might like to write down any feelings they now had when they got home. We would take up these issues at our next introductory meeting.

The next day I wrote to all the participants thus:

Dear

I thought I would write to everyone in the Active Learning group following our session on Tuesday evening for two reasons. First, since I had suggested that we each write down some of our thoughts and feelings to share, I wanted to try to clarify some of my own by writing to you. Secondly, I felt that the session ended rather abruptly with many of us (including myself) feeling somewhat uncertain about where we were going. So I shall try to work out some of my own feelings and impressions in this letter, recognizing that it might seem very different for you.

My first thoughts concern this question of being clear about where we are going. I thought that I was clear that the aim of the course is: to explore, experientially, the rhetoric of active learning in particular in relation to the idea of negotiating our own learning and exercising control over our own activity.

But although I was clear about that aim (which might not have been clear to you?) I was not, and am still not, sure about how we achieve it. I could, for example, suggest a series of workshop activities which we then reflect upon to help us understand how we negotiate and communicate with each other.

The only trouble with this strategy is that if I suggest the workshop activities, are they really negotiated? Wouldn't people just follow my suggestions because I was the course leader? In which case, wouldn't this be just another form of didactic learning, with everyone following the tutor's course programme?

On the other hand, if I don't suggest how we should proceed, how will we come to any decision? For it seemed that there was a wide divergence of feeling amongst the group between those who wanted a clear structure provided for them to work within, and those who preferred the uncertainty of not knowing quite where we're going until we get there.

While this does seem to be a real dilemma for us, I think it is very relevant for understanding active learning. Often when I have worked with students and tried to develop active learning approaches I have encountered the same problem. Some people want the kind of clearly defined objectives set for them as normally happens with more didactic teaching; others are prepared to stay with the kind of unpredictability and uncertainty which normally accompanies a more exploratory approach. This difference doesn't matter too much, perhaps, if the students are working individually, for then some just follow more structured paths than others. The problem arises in work in groups, when the differing needs for structure can't both be met.

I feel that one boundary condition of this course is that we should attempt to work as a group (although at times we may not want to be all together). If this is agreed, we then have to work out how to resolve our differing need for a structure. And if we decide that we need more structure, we have to agree about where this structure should come from (for example, should I provide it? should someone else 'facilitate' a process for arriving at it?)

You may feel that this is all very confusing, and that it would be better if we just got on with some active learning activity, of whatever kind, to give us something clear to work on. In part, that's how I feel, and I could certainly provide some such activity (and no doubt others in the group could too). But in part I also feel that the confusion of the situation is actually something valuable to learn from. What we are grappling with is the difficulty we find when we come to question the assumptions we make about teaching and learning. If we just ignore this problem (for example, by deciding that I should devise a programme of activity), we shall miss out on an opportunity to experience what happens when we question some of these assumptions. And that, I feel, would be to fail in the aim of the course which is to test out some of our basic beliefs about teaching and learning. For if active learning is anything significant, it is an approach which is founded upon a radical change in the way we think about the relationships between teachers, learners, and the subject matter.

I don't know whether this makes any sense to you. I look forward to hearing how you are feeling about it and any ideas you have about how we might proceed, when we meet again on Tuesday 24 April (7.00–9.00). I would like it if, after the formal session, we go off to the local pub so that we can get to know a bit more about each other in more relaxed surroundings.

I hope you have a good holiday over Easter.

With best wishes,

Second Introductory Session: 24 April 7.00–9.00pm

The session seemed altogether less tense. Perhaps my letter had helped to allay some fears. Perhaps the approach of the weekend, only three days away, made people feel that they were committed now, so they would try to make the most of the experience.

One person who, in the previous session, had expressed his worry about the lack of a plan now said that he felt the course was like a trip on a bus, to be enjoyed in itself without worrying too much about where it is going. (Someone else added that it was even more exciting not to have a bus driver!) Others, however, still seemed to feel anxious.

There was some discussion about my role. A suggestion was made that we should make a formal agreement that, during the weekend, I would not be expected to take on a 'tutor' role. Someone else said that such an agreement would not amount to much and that, if it was felt that my role needed discussing, we should do that rather than hide behind a formal agreement. There seemed to be emerging a general acceptance that 'tutorly' expectations would not be made of me during the weekend. I said that I welcomed this and that, during the weekend, I didn't want to be discussing the writing which people might want assessed as part of the MEd programme. If needed, I would help with that after the weekend.

The conversation turned to thinking about what people might bring to the weekend. Flip charts and coloured pens? Bottles of wine? Cards to play with? Was this going to be a working weekend or a party? Did it matter anyway, couldn't they both be forms of active learning? I put my foot down at the suggestion that we might play *Trivial Pursuit*, but was firmly put in my place by someone who said that since I was no longer 'tutor' I shouldn't be so heavy. It's just that

I can't stand *Trivial Pursuit*. This seemed to be an appropriate point to go to the pub and get to know each other better.

I now felt much more relaxed than after the first session. I think others were too. It seemed that we now at least shared an expectation that we didn't know what to expect, and that there was no point in looking to me to get it sorted.

There must still, however, have been apprehensions. Is this just going to be a weekend party? But if it is, are these the people I would choose to have a party with? Or will it be endless intellectual discussions which are out of my depth? Will there be any exciting new ideas or will it be painfully boring? Or painful in some other way? Such thoughts must have occurred to many of us.

At this stage, however, I felt there was a shared understanding that, for the duration of the weekend, I would not act as a leader in any way. I would take no responsibility for the processes by which we made decisions or the outcomes of them. Apart from my deciding when the first session should begin on the Friday, and the last one end on the Sunday, I would have no special responsibility for when we 'worked' and when we didn't.

The Residential Weekend: Northern College 27–29 April

Friday evening
The views from Northern College, an impressive early nineteenth century country house, give a feeling of spaciousness and command over the surrounding countryside. Its gardens are famous for their varieties of mature rhododendrons and for the azaleas which were at their best this weekend. Even the weather was perfect.

Coming from work, we arrived in ones and twos, parked cars, registered, found our bedrooms, wandered in to an evening meal. The start of a residential; familiar to me but perhaps strange to some of the others. I felt excited, but also apprehensive. Forty-four hours is a long time to spend with ten people you don't know. What if we discover we don't like each other? Do you have to like people to work well with them?

We assembled for the first session at 7.30pm. Apart from meal times, this was the only fixed part of the agenda. Comfortable chairs were arranged in a circle. I can't remember who decided to move the furniture, but little decisions like that seemed important. Conversation started falteringly. Had we 'started' yet? Who was to say?

Soon we seemed to be listening to each other and contributions were made to get the discussion going, nervously perhaps. What were we going to do? Someone suggested a game which involved physical contact. Someone else said they disliked the idea; that if everyone else wanted to play it, that was alright by them, but they wouldn't join in. Other suggestions were made and rejected. How would we reach any decision? At least we were able to decide upon a finishing time after which we would be able to have a drink. There's nothing like real need to force the decision making powers of a group!

Eventually a suggestion was taken up, or grasped upon, as giving us some direction. It involved us each saying where, and with whom, we would like to spend our 'ideal' day. We each contributed and thereby revealed just a little of ourselves. The last person to speak said she would like to be here and with these people. This was the ideal.

That made me feel a lot better.

The conversation over the two hours that the session lasted was difficult. The silences clearly felt awkward to some. Frustration and even anger seemed only a little below the surface as we struggled to discuss how we would work together. By the end of the session we had no plan of action, although we had agreed when we would meet the next morning.

Forming the right relationships for working together on our task was not an easy process. Coming from a variety of professional backgrounds — a primary school teacher, college of further education lecturer, occupational therapist, and so on — we shared no obvious professional concern except for our interest in learning. During the session we did not spend time swapping accounts about our working lives. It seemed that we needed to know about each other as people, not just as roles. People are more difficult to get to know than roles, and more vulnerable.

Trainers often talk about 'ice-breaking' as being the aim of a first session. This session wasn't an ice-breaker. On the contrary, it felt more as though we were trying to remain on top of the ice for fear of what might happen if it did break.

After the session we split up, some people going to the bar, others remaining in the room to talk things over. The informal sharing of feelings, which could not yet be expressed when we were all together, no doubt led to the development of friendships and alliances. By the end of the evening we all met up again to share wine and make plans for a walk before breakfast the next day.

By the end of the day I felt that we were a group of very different individuals. We were not readily going to set aside our own needs for some supposed common good.

Saturday

These differences emerged forcefully at the beginning of the first session on Saturday morning. Someone said that they felt the weekend would be a waste of time unless we got down to some clear task. Threats were made to leave. I felt my heartbeat quicken as I envisaged us disintegrating.

The feelings of dissension were talked through and, before long, a suggestion for a joint activity emerged: we would make a group picture on a very large sheet of paper. Two people declined to join in, saying they didn't see the point, but would be happy to observe.

I felt that the 'decliners' were responded to sensitively. Rather than making them feel rejected for not wanting to join in, they were encouraged to observe so that we could then draw upon their observations later. Thinking this over later, I thought that this showed an important insight about negotiation. Too often I'm inclined to try to work towards agreement between everyone in a group rather than recognize the importance of differences in people's abilities and preferences. Perhaps negotiation isn't always about reaching agreements but about facing and making the most of differences. Interestingly, when we later talked about our drawing and our purpose in doing this, the person who had not joined in realized that she had not really understood the aim of the activity, and that if she had done, she would have joined us. Another interesting lesson in negotiation.

The task had helped to draw us together. It had provided a shared learning experience to which we could refer in further discussion. But it only temporarily solved what seemed, for some, to be our major difficulty: deciding what to do next. It seemed to me that some people hoped for the weekend to be a series of 'active learning activities' from which we would learn about active learning. The processes of deciding what the activities were to be was something which should be accomplished as simply as possible so that we could get on with the learning. For others, there was emerging a somewhat different expectation. While there might be 'activities' which we wanted to share, the real work was centred in the more messy process of exploring how we felt about what was happening 'here and now' as we negotiated, shared our anxieties, exposed our vulnerability. For these people, this approach would be more valuable in helping us to understanding ourselves as communicators and learners.

It would be foolish to suggest that everyone adopted one or the other of these two perspectives. For other people, this may not even have been a central issue.

Later in the morning it became clear that others also felt there to be some important difference between us. The conversation had been very explorative with a good deal of uncomfortable feelings expressed, but little progress on any defined task. Then someone who, it had seemed to me wanted a more definite structure of activities, said that she suspected that others knew something which she didn't. She didn't see the point of this kind of talk, but it was obvious to her that others in the group did. What were they getting out of it? What did they know that she didn't? Was she just being thick? Was there some hidden agenda which she wasn't aware of?

I didn't feel like her, and I'm sure many others didn't. For me the conversation was very significant. But so often — at parties, committee meetings and so on — I do feel like her. It's not that I don't understand what is being said, but that I don't really see the point of all the talk. It doesn't really interest me although it clearly does engage other people. When that happens, I rarely say how I feel. I either leave, if I can, or attempt to change the conversation, or just put up with it. But what was happening here was quite different. She was owning up to how she felt, at the risk of making herself look silly. If the replies she received from others didn't actually solve her difficulties, at least she was taken seriously which would have been of some support to her and others who might have had similar feelings.

As the day progressed this preparedness to take the risk of exposing feelings increased. Someone else, with great difficulty, told us how he feared that he would not have anything valuable to contribute to the discussions because he didn't feel that he was very good with words. By the time he had thought of what to say the idea seemed trivial, or it no longer seemed relevant. It seemed to him that others were cleverer than he was when it came to this sort of thing. I guess most of us have felt like this at times, but how often are we able to admit it, at the moment when we feel it, to a group of people with whom we are committed to working?

By the end of the day I felt that we were more open with each other, more ready to express the kinds of feelings which, the previous evening, would probably have remained below the surface. And if this was so, we had built a better basis for sharing and negotiating in a way which didn't mean we had to hide our individual needs in order to meet those of the group. Learning was therefore becoming more possible.

It had been a long and intense day. Apart from breaks for meals and two hours free in the afternoon, we had spent from 9.30am until 9.30pm sitting in a circle talking to each other. But had we got to know each other? I still knew almost nothing about anyone's professional background or family and social life. But that no longer seemed to matter.

The rest of the day was spent in the bar, playing silly games over bottles of wine and consuming tea and toast until late into the night. Fortunately, no one had brought *Trivial Pursuit*. We could be much more inventive than that.

Sunday

As we gathered for the first session of the morning, conversations died down and we were soon sitting in silence. Perhaps one or two people still found silences difficult, but I think many of us appreciated them. To me it seemed appropriate, at the beginning of the day's work, to reflect quietly together. Since no one had responsibility for starting sessions, perhaps we were each wondering whether we had anything we wanted to say to start things off. Or do some people always just assume that it will be someone else who takes the risk of starting things off? As the silence lengthened it made whatever was going to be said seem more significant.

There must have been several interludes of silence during our time together on Sunday morning. But they felt different. Sometimes it would just seem like a natural break, a pause between one theme and another, like between the movements of a piano sonata. Or an opportunity to listen to the blackbird outside the window. At others the silence would provide a few moments to think about what had just been said. Yet others would provide a minute during which someone plucked up the courage to say something they had been wanting to say for a long time, but had not dared to.

In such an atmosphere listening was very acute. No words were wasted; whatever anyone said was accepted, thought about and responded to with or without words. Rarely did anyone interrupt what was being said, there was no feeling of people waiting for a space to say their bit. There seemed to be an intense concentration upon the moment in hand. Ideas and feelings were fully shared with none of the 'defending of positions' which seems to characterize so many group discussions.

The content of the talk also seemed to change during the morning. Increasingly, we would concentrate on a very specific problem which someone would bring up. Towards the end of the last session one person, with great difficulty, started to talk about something which had distressed her for years, but which she had felt she was not really able to talk about or to come to terms with. As she spoke, she became unable to control herself, and perhaps no longer wanted to control herself. She wept, then got up and left the room saying that she was sorry, but she could not stay.

I'm sure that was a very difficult moment for everyone. Someone said that she felt that this kind of thing was very dangerous, someone else disagreed. At that moment I felt very responsible. Had this really all got out of control? What was I going to do about it? Should I also leave the room, to go and comfort the person who had left? Would she want that anyway? Inspite of what we had agreed and achieved in terms of being an unled group, I felt that it now depended upon my actions. The crunch had now come. I had to do something.

I waited. The silence perhaps lasted no longer than a minute or two, but it seemed like an hour. I just wanted us all to trust each other.

The door opened quietly and the person who had left us returned to sit down. She was hugged by someone sitting next to her. Quieter now, but still with great feeling, she spoke, saying that she was glad this had happened. She had said what she had wanted to say. We had all enabled and supported her to do this, and this was important to her. I had helped her to come to terms with something which had been a source of difficulties for a long time.

The group now felt very warm and close. During the next half hour there were more silences. Two or three other people also shared, with great feeling, things that they were finding painful. Support was offered silently, or by a touch, or by encouragement.

After another silence, I felt that it must now be the end of our weekend sessions. In fact we were already half an hour late for lunch. Someone said they would like us to write down, together, some notes about what we have experienced and learnt during the morning. This was quickly agreed by everyone, a felt tip pen and large sheet of paper were found and someone offered to be scribe. In ten minutes we worked very fast, each offering ideas and enlarging upon each other's. Notes were made on the large sheet:

No-one will tell me when it's safe
Taking risks
Honesty
Decisions taken about risks — you take them not alcohol
Learning changes us
Support/need to feel supported at times
Risky saying what I need from the group
Asking for help
Clarification of task

*The need to tell for the group's sake outweighs the fear of taking risks
— obligation
Individuals need time to get to know each other before becoming a
group
Empathy is difficult — competitive environment militates against these
types of development
Rescuing each other
Getting to know yourself even if you didn't want to
Alliances
Respect
Identity: loss of identity to the group is a fear rather than an actual loss
Sense of belonging
Evaluation — 1   Attempted change in practice
            2   Personal development
            3   Changing relationships
                Difficult to assess these
Constraints: Working within national/local guidelines and standards*

Someone offered to type up the list and circulate it at our next, follow
up, meeting back at the university. It was also agreed that, at that
meeting, we would report to each other on how the weekend's
experience had influenced our personal and professional lives during
the intervening ten days.

The work was finished, for now.

We walked downstairs for our final meal. Someone began pushing
tables together so that we could all sit around one table. I didn't feel
hungry.

Saying goodbye to each other after lunch and coffee took a long
time. For me, finishing can be as difficult as beginning.

First Follow-up Session at the University: 8 May

The conversation started slowly. It was ten days since we were last
together, and no longer in the intimate surroundings which we had
made our own during the weekend. People told of their immediate
reactions to the experience and how they now felt about it, reporting
on how it had influenced things. For one it had changed how he felt
about and behaved in an interview for a new job. (It later turned out
that he was successful in the interview.) Another told about how it had
led her to change the way her headteacher related to her. Another

about how it made her realize that she had not been looking after her own needs in her personal life, only everyone else's, and that she was now beginning to do something about that. For one or two, the experience had been powerful at the time but its effect had worn off once they had become reacclimatized to 'normal' professional relationships at work.

What began to emerge from our discussion was the question of how we were going to transfer what we had gained from the weekend to our continuing professional lives. While it seemed that our way of relating and working in the group was now strong, and it would be good if we could continue working together, what was important was no longer the group, but our wider lives.

The other concern which now loomed up was how we were going to represent our learning over the weekend for the purpose of assessment on the university course. After some discussion of this it was decided that each of us would write a fairly immediate response to the experience. Copies of this writing would be shared at our final follow-up meeting. It was also decided that we would tape record a conversation, at that final meeting, in which we would, as a group, reflect upon the work. This collection of writing and the tape recording would then be a resource available for anyone who wished to submit work for assessment.

A further problem, however, arose in relation to this plan. The way we had worked together over the course had been genuinely cooperative. A 'culture' had emerged in which, consistent with the principles of active learning as we understood them, each of us took responsibility for our own learning, and no-one was in any special position to make judgments about the learning of others. How then could I, as a member of the group, act as a judge of the work each person produced? Some people felt this was not a problem. Others felt that it was, but this was a necessary compromise we had to make in the face of the normal institutional demands for accountability of accreditation. One person said that she would evaluate her own written product, providing her own 'tutor's comments' if necessary, since she didn't see how I could act as a judge.

I agreed to discuss this matter, on behalf of the group, with colleagues in the university, so that I could advise them at the next meeting.

Final Follow-up Session at the University: 7 June

Following discussions with other staff, I suggested that people really had three alternatives:

(i)   they could simply submit work to be assessed by me, as course tutor, in the normal way;

(ii) they could devise their own criteria for assessment and evaluate their own work accordingly. In this case, the work would still have to be submitted to me for me to make a judgment about the appropriateness of their criteria and the validity of their evaluation;

(iii) they could choose not to submit work for assessment. This would be quite acceptable and not seen as any kind of failure.

Discussing this question of assessment was uncomfortable. Having enjoyed an opportunity to learn together with the group I now felt I had returned to the roles of tutor and bureaucrat. Whether I liked it or not, I now represented the institution which awards credit for the work done on the course. As such, I could no longer see myself as an equal participant. The inevitable interface between personal learning and institutional accreditation of learning was now focused in this change of my role.

Most of the meeting was spent in some kind of evaluatory dis-cussion of the course, which was recorded as we had agreed. This was organized by one of the participants who also offered to copy tapes of the discussion for circulation amongst the group. I think there was a general feeling by the end that this discussion did little to capture the flavour of the experience or what we had gained from it. To me, it seemed somewhat artificial to evaluate the process at the end in this way, for the whole process had been one of continual evaluation and reflection.

The meeting adjourned to the local pub. By the end of the evening a further informal meeting had been organized. Some friendships had been made and we enjoyed talking together, but the intense experience of the weekend would not be repeated in such informal surroundings.

Part II: Reflections on the Experience

Introduction

After the first follow-up session, it was decided that everyone might write a short piece (a couple of sides was suggested) in which they reflected upon the course. No one suggested any form or focus for this writing, it being thought better that everyone should respond in whatever way they felt appropriate. Everyone did write a piece. They varied in length between about 300 and 2000 words and also in style.

There was no suggestion at this point that the writing would have any audience beyond ourselves. It was not intended for assessment or publication purposes. Each of us, writing fairly immediately and for each other, jumped from one theme to another according to what seemed important at the time. I have therefore reorganized the writings, extracting themes which keep cropping up and presenting the work in extracts thematically. This had inevitably involved some selection (and therefore judgment) on my part. I shall, however, keep my own interpretation of these writings to a minimum, in an attempt to allow the participants to speak in their own voices.

The themes to emerge from the writings concerned the expectations which people brought to the course; the processes of negotiation; group support; group leadership; and the outcomes of the experience. Almost all the writing related to one or the other of these themes, so I shall present it under these general headings.

Expectations

Kath: I thought I knew what active learning was about. However I also felt that I would like to know more. I was apprehensive about the weekend and worried about whether I would cope intellectually. The first meeting did little to reassure me as I really felt I needed definite objectives to work towards.

Kath was not the only one to admit that she had been worried about her ability to cope intellectually, perhaps not an unusual experience for people at the beginning of a University course:

Ellen: On arrival there began the initial first impressions. Thoughts go through your head — who will be on the course? What will the other people be like? Will I like them? Will I get on with them? Will they be more intellectual than me? etc., etc.

Liz: My only real fear was that I might not be able to participate or add anything of value to a discussion if we became entrenched in heavy discussions relating to politics, philosophy or something of that ilk, in that in those areas I don't believe myself to be a clear thinker or one who can voice lucid views or opinions. I lack confidence in myself and believe that others will think me a fool.

But after the course, Liz felt very differently.

Kath's other worry about needing definite objectives, or a clear idea of what the task was to be, was also reflected in Jill's writing.

Jill: When I met the group for the first time I felt very self-conscious. I was surprised that we weren't given clear directions as to what was to take place — little did I know that part of active learning was to negotiate and in fact that's what was actually happening already!

Having met everyone and still not really knowing what was going to happen — the weekend loomed nearer — all would be revealed I hoped!

Again I was extremely apprehensive about the weekend and started to think of reasons why I didn't want to be there.

and in Ray's:

Ray: There seemed to be, despite the tutor's clear exposition of the experimental nature of the process, a need to know what the task was and an expectation that it should be externally provided.

For Richard, the problems of a lack of structure at the outset were, to some extent, overcome during the preparatory sessions before the weekend:

Richard: At our initial meeting I found it difficult to come to terms with a learning experience that seemed to have little or no structure. By the time of our second meeting I had gone some way into coming to terms with this, seeing the weekend ahead as an experience for the experience's sake (if that makes any sense).

But not everyone was anxious about the lack of structure.

Ellen: I think that (a local authority in-service programme) had prepared me very well for this unit of work on

active learning in that at this stage I felt few of the mis-
givings which it seemed were apparent in some other
members of the group. Some people were worrying
about what the actual task was, what we were going to
do, what we were going to learn about and whether or
not by the end of the weekend there would be material
enough to write the dreaded assignment and hence get
another pass along the way to a degree . . . or maybe
I am of a nature less inclined to worry about something which at that time was still some way off in the
future . . . I felt quite positive and looking forward to
a weekend away in beautiful new surroundings . . . I
can remember saying . . . 'Let's just enjoy the weekend
. . . life is all one big active learn anyway.' I think that
perhaps sums up how I was feeling at the time.

Liz: I arrived on the Friday evening of our weekend together feeling a little nervous, excited, full of anticipation and yet not really knowing what it was that I was
about to embark upon. I was prepared to wait and see
what developed and felt from the start that that would
be the active learning itself.

This feeling of not knowing what we were about to embark upon was
a natural precursor to a period of negotiation.

The Process of Negotiation

Theresa: Decision making — This was difficult! Even deciding what time our sessions would stop and start was
hard. We would begin to discuss, get diverted, then
go back to it, try again, and decide who most people
agreed with. The most satisfying decision was that
we didn't all need to agree to do anything.

Another way of looking at 'we didn't all need to agree' is 'not allowing
myself to be coerced', as Ray puts it:

Ray: Attending this open weekend I did not have an agenda
which I wished to bring forward. I had not prepared
any activities as such, however I became quickly aware
of the things that matter to me in conversation with

others . . . I was acutely aware of the things which did not interest me and the difficulty of being polite, but not allowing myself to be coerced or pressured by the group to conform to activities or points of focus . . .

Ellen, however, felt on Saturday morning that to conform was preferable to opting out.

Ellen: The first session on Saturday morning cemented together the group as a whole. Although the task of drawing on a piece of paper was perhaps irrelevant it actually served the purpose of getting the group talking together as everybody participated in the discussion. I myself was not particularly thrilled at the thought of drawing on a piece of paper but was not prepared to be one of the people who refused to join in the task.

Alliances were formed during this negotiating phase, whether or not we chose to conform.

Sarah: People forming alliances seemed to be very important. It increased the safety of the group for people, and encouraged people to get together and sort out or process what they were experiencing. Possibly it provided opportunities for people to vent feelings of frustration or anger which they would not have felt alright to share with the whole group. What surprised me was that alliances did not seem to disrupt the group or form opposing camps. People's alliances seemed to be acknowledged yet not perceived as a threat to group cohesion.

Acknowledging these alliances enabled Pauline to gain from individual differences in the group.

Pauline: While my first impressions regarding those individuals that I would relate to more easily than others did not change during the weekend, what did change was my easing up and willingness to take on board people who I would not normally associate with. In these people I found a range of strengths and weaknesses and whole difference in ways of looking at things.

Working with these differences, is perhaps a way in which we were able to reach out across social barriers, as Sarah suggests:

> *Sarah:* Negotiating learning goals and processes in a group rather than individually required that the group needed to get to know each other. In order to be able to negotiate we seemed to benefit from getting to trust each other, to take risks, removing our masks, letting go of preconceptions and stereotypes about each other, exposing our humanness, and our ability to care for each other, our personal fear of being rejected or devalued. We managed to reach out across barriers of gender, class, and belief systems or politics.

Working through this process of negotiation appeared to bring the group closer together.

Group Support

Here Richard describes how he experienced this process of growth in the trust between people.

> *Richard:* I felt that what the group was doing was to establish a common ground in order to produce a working environment. In order to do this it would be necessary for the group to know something about each other, not just the external trappings of each other's lives but more about the 'inner' person . . .
>
> I felt in a difficult position: the group were wondering what I had to say, what I had decided. I didn't feel confident enough to tell the group, I didn't trust the group. If the group was to make progress there must be trust. The obligation to the group became more important, more powerful, than not speaking . . . I think it was about this time that the group started to have the feeling of 'oneness' . . . I very much felt now that the group had passed from the stage of looking closely at each other and that each member of the group was, with the trust and support of the group, looking very closely at themselves, trying to come to terms with their own inabilities and patterns of behaviour.

By the Sunday session I felt that the trust and support from the group was so strong that individuals were being completely open to each other, or almost completely. It seemed that the group could now discuss anything about itself or any individual without anyone feeling that they would have to retreat, the way they may have done thirty-six hours before. To my mind the group was now very much one group and ready to tackle any learning experience that it may decide as a group to do.

We were close mentally and I felt at the beginning of something rather than at the end. It had taken the group some forty-two hours to reach this point.

Liz also wrote about this as a process of change, and described how she experienced the quality of group support.

Liz: I felt that the support was so great at times that it was like a fence enclosing me, keeping me safe, allowing me to make choices in an unthreatening environment, giving me time to explore my inner feelings. I experienced the 'closing in' and 'releasing' aspects of that support when I no longer needed its strength in the same way. I felt that if I had tried to I could have reached out and touched it, it felt so real. It didn't imprison and yet it did, it bound us together until some of us felt secure enough to off load and express feelings which had lain hidden and unvoiced for some time. Unconscious feelings which hurt and shape our characters were awakened and voiced in front of people who others might have called strangers.

But Ellen, recognizing the empathy in the group, nevertheless felt herself starting to withdraw.

Ellen: When Pauline became upset by memories, she found two people, Liz and later Richard, who greatly shared the same feelings, perhaps due to having been through similar circumstances. I feel there was also a great deal of understanding and empathy from the other group members. At this stage I feel I started to withdraw . . .

77

> I began to feel a turn away from the group, and during this time I actually started to feel like an outsider. I felt other people were moving forward and leaving me behind. Maybe this means I do not give of myself very easily, although having said that I appreciate it was not an easy thing for the others to do. I also felt inadequate in that at one time Liz, who was sitting next to me, was upset and I felt totally unable to offer any comfort or to say anything to ease the situation.

If Ellen was feeling left behind, Theresa saw people's expressions of feelings as a step forward.

> *Theresa*: When Kath and Jill talked about how they felt on Saturday morning it was a powerful step forward. When Ray told Pauline how he felt about the comments she made about what he said — NOBODY DIED . . . We changed, grew together, grew closer together, became capable of more. Things were done for the sake of the group, because of the group. Each time someone was able to take a risk, and make themselves vulnerable by revealing something of themselves, it became easier for others to do the same . . . People talked about deeply personal things. This happened in a short time, and individuals did this for themselves, took risks, looked after themselves, allowed it to happen.

and for Jill this growing closeness was a relief.

> *Jill*: I realized that during that Sunday morning session a feeling of friendship and togetherness had really developed as a result of the weekend. The tears and emotions that followed confirmed this. I felt a closeness with everyone and to some extent a feeling of relief.

While much of this writing expresses excitement about what we did during the weekend, underlying this is a sense of struggle and, at times, pain. This makes the role of the 'leader' or 'teacher' even more fraught.

The weekend developed out of a negotiated agreement that I would not have any particular responsibilities with regard to leadership during the residential experience. Whether I liked it or not, however, my responsibility as the person who had drawn together the group for this purpose can not be avoided. To use Richard's analogy, I was the 'bus driver' on this journey, even if I had negotiated with the group that I would not sit in the driving seat.

Group Leadership

This is the most difficult issue for me to address through the words of the other participants, since it related to my own actions during the weekend. I shall, however, attempt to report what other participants said without comment.

Only three people (apart from myself) addressed the question of my own role directly. This seems surprising to me since one of the main concerns of the weekend seemed to be to test out the active learning rhetoric concerning the relationship between teacher and learner. Others may not have commented because they didn't think it was important; or because they really felt that the weekend itself was 'leaderless' (and it was just the weekend they were writing about, not the course as a whole) and so the issue didn't arise; or because they would have found it difficult to be open about their feelings to me concerning my role. Or perhaps, in the writing which had already been reported here, the issues of leadership are implicit and adequately reflect their feelings on this matter.

> *Ray*: Much of the anxiety of the need for direction and tutor control I believe has historical roots in the educational experiences of us all . . . I believe we experienced a common doubt about the role and the responsibility of the leader/teacher, but not necessarily a solution, for though the tensions diminished to some extent during the weekend itself, they reasserted themselves with the need to make decisions about accreditation, and at that point the issue is one which will always remain where there is an expectation that someone is provider of 'knowledge' or the opportunity through which knowledge can be acquired.

This 'need to make decisions about accreditation' refers to the meeting after the weekend, at the university, a meeting during which Pauline also sensed a change in my role.

Pauline: I was intrigued by Stephen's role last Tuesday. From not really wanting to get involved in the whole 'assignment' debate, I felt a shift to wanting an outcome, that is, he wanted an outcome. There was a move to pull people together and yet one of the important acceptances during the weekend was of individual differences. This led me to thinking about the reality of the the situation we had found ourselves in. Carl Rogers once wrote. 'I cannot teach anyone anything, I can only provide an environment in which he (sic) can learn.'

The environment was managed for me on Tuesday, and I am aware of the need for this. To create the right ambiance in which to learn and grow, can be very difficult . . . If we have to work within a system that demands certain performances and results then we have to acknowledge these, but work towards changing the way in which learning takes place. For me, this is part of what active learning is all about. It's taking given circumstances and working with the individuals involved to empower them and not to make them the slaves of the constraints imposed from outside. These constraints could be anything from the examination board syllabus to personal relationships that are restrictive.

Ray takes up this point about the teacher/leader working within the constraints, and the need to be open about this.

Ray: At best the leader/teacher can be open about the limits within which the 'learning' can be experienced, and offer the opportunity for active learning to take place, suffer the loneliness of the profession, and trust in the process. Within that framework the responsibility genuinely becomes that of the learner for the choice of subject/area of enquiry, for decisions on the form in which this learning will be evidenced, if at all . . . I believe that despite the limits of the system, the opportunity I have experienced has been worthwhile in allowing me to reconstruct my knowledge and understanding, and is allowing me to imagine possibilities for the future which are filled less with dread and more with anticipation.

Sarah reflects at some length on the question of leadership during the weekend, leaving me much to think about:

Sarah: I was amazed and excited by the way we all took responsibility for the group and the weekend, responding to individual's needs and responses, and coping well when it got sticky. The sticky bits were even utilized to herald new turning points. It made me question my current practices as leader of certain groups and I have since been successful at being much more risky in sharing power and responsibility . . .

Using Stephen as a model I was able to explore my own ambiguities about being in the role of tutor or therapist. I appreciated his sharing of what it was like for him during the weekend, and I appreciated the risks he was taking, in letting go of control, attempting to find a way of equal participation, and illuminating his own needs or wants within the group. I am still not clear about some issues.

Status — Coping with having dual status, of being in a position of power, the marker of assignments, the authority on this topic, the one who is paid to be there (money can be seen as part of society valuing someone), the position of being a university lecturer. Maybe these are only in my head, ie. someone only has status if we agree to confer it, or if it is cultural or traditional, if we collude with it.

Friendship — Within the group several friendships were made, and these seemed to enrich people's experience of the group. But I have a feeling of unease about whether it is alright for a tutor to show comraderie to any individuals more than others, which I felt was happening. And yet if the tutor is an equal participant why should he or she not also enjoy new alliances? It is something about me wanting to be labelled teacher's pet, and still my lurking expectation that the tutor should hold a special responsibility for the group as a whole, in case something 'serious' goes wrong. This would mean the tutor standing slightly outside the group and not getting too close to any individuals or small group. Possibly this is about something that I would find it hard to let go of myself, to completely give up all responsibility for a group of people I had been instrumental in bringing together.

The question of the leader's own needs is raised by Pauline:

> *Pauline*: I have become more curious about Stephen's role in all this. I think one of the reasons he takes part in things like this is to try and sort out problems and confusions that he faces in his own life.

But Sarah suggests that the tutor's growth might be as important as anyone else's.

> *Sarah*: I think that leaders tend to get isolated, and estranged from the group. We all need support whatever our role. Whether the group can support the leader, I think depends on how much the group members have attention outside their own concerns, how much equality there is. The group's purpose is not to help the leader explore their personal development, but why can't the leader's growth be as important as everyone else's?

Here Sarah suggests a collaborative approach in which everyone is learning together regardless of their role in the group. This challenges accepted notions of leadership.

By the end of the weekend, we had clearly achieved a degree of closeness, empathy and collaboration. But what does this achievement amount to? What would be its value to our continuing personal and professional lives? Even if the process had achieved this 'satisfactory' conclusion by the end of the weekend, what had we learned from the process that we could take away with us?

The Outcomes

The power of the experience was reported in much of the writing. Its significance, though, depends upon the extent to which it is part of a continuing process of change and development. Pauline keeps returning to this point:

> *Pauline*: Spending a weekend with strangers and ending up feeling a bond between myself and them is an

unusual experience. It took some doing. There is more to come from this and I feel very strongly that the weekend was part of a process that, for me, has implications for the way I relate to others. It must make me a more effective communicator. I have been aware of listening more intently to people since the weekend. I have also been aware of a diminishing of the need to 'provide answers' . . .

That the weekend is part of a continuum is essential. Being given the time and space to explore thoughts, feelings, ideas, anxieties and purposes was incredible and a valuable jumping off point . . .

One of the things that I have been able to do much more effectively is to recognize another's point of view and respect that without wishing to try to make sense of it within my own frame of reference . . .

I believe that an important aspect of active learning is giving others the opportunity to search out what they genuinely would like to do and how they would like to respond, not only to the individuals, but in groups and to issues and situations that they might face. For me this is very much part of an ongoing process. I feel that this can be done within the system, but obviously not to the same extent that it could given fewer constraints. There is a challenge there and it's about the way we operate as individuals.

While Pauline sees the constraints of the system as offering us a challenge, Richard is less optimistic about the possibility of developing these ideas in the 'educational system':

Richard: Could a less interested group with less concentrated contact time ever reach the stage of being ready to decide the content of its learning experience? If it can, it would take far too long, more time than the educational system could afford to give and any change in the group structure would mean that the whole group would have to develop again.

The question of whether the value of the experience will remain and be developed, or be lost, is taken up by others.

Kath: ... for a few days I was a better listener. If I've lost that then I should strive to regain it. Thinking about it and recalling recent events, perhaps it's not lost, just internalized.

Jill: The process had done something for me — I felt different — it lasted for only a few days. After being back at college for 2 or 3 days unfortunately the peaceful feelings disappeared — outside influences had taken over ...

I think the weekend made me a good listener and certainly sensitive to the feelings of others — made me accept and respect the opinions of others without question.

The value of listening, which Pauline, Kath and Jill remarked upon, emerged in much of the writing. Here Theresa also makes this point and develops it further.

Theresa: I seemed to be listening to people talk about a different range of things. This has not only been at work, but also in the pub! I have also talked about a different range of things. I've said more about things I don't usually talk about, and less about things I actually prefer to keep for myself.

I have changed the way my headteacher behaves towards me. Not by refusing to say things she doesn't like to hear, but by putting her into situations when it would be too churlish for her to be unfriendly. And when I crashed my car she brought me flowers.

I have become braver, and more creative, about telling people things they don't want to hear — or turning them into things they do want to hear. I have been surprised by how effective 'I don't like that' is.

I have given myself more time. I've had some material for two years, and now it's stitched — it meant not doing other things, that I wanted to do less. I've spent much more of my time not doing anything. Only thinking!

I'm aware of learning in different ways. There have been some painting workshops at school, and I have found that I have been able to paint some ideas to a conclusion.

> I might be finding it easier to be wrong! I've
> been able to stop myself making lists of reasons why
> things are someone else's fault, accept responsibility
> for what I've done, and not bother too much about
> guilt. This is closely tied to my attempts to suspend
> judgment, to stop identifying good/bad, nice/nasty.

Theresa's idea of giving more time for herself was reflected by Ellen:

Ellen: Certainly one major factor I think is the importance of
actually taking time for oneself in order to reflect, to
think, to ponder over what has actually been happening, in all aspects of life.

and by Liz who sees it as part of a process which enables her to value
herself:

Liz: Since our weekend and subsequent meeting I have continued to learn about myself. It hasn't been 'active' in the
way some of us expected this sort of learning to be. It's
been very peaceful, relaxed, painful at times. I feel I have
gained a sort of inner strength, maybe it's just a little self
confidence, I don't know. I have made decisions about
my life that are important ones which began to form in
my mind as Saturday of our weekend progressed. I am
me. I am a person in my own rights. I need space and
time to myself in order to set my stall straight. I can
listen and say nothing if I don't wish to contribute, without feeling threatened. But most of all I have realized
that I am not a fool and that my ideas and opinions
(providing they are well thought out) are as valuable as
anyone else's, and that means a lot to me.

That this idea of increased self-worth is gained at a cost in terms of
struggle, and facing difficult things about ourselves, is indicated by
Ray's postscript to his writing in which he asserts the validity of active
learning. He also makes the difficult statement that valuable learning
may not always be enjoyable.

Ray: I did not enjoy the experience of the weekend or the
meetings before or after. I found them valuable then
and now. I experienced struggle, much more than I can

remember in a school learning sense. My struggles then were boredom, disinterest. Here the struggles were about facing things I didn't have the energy or courage to face, imaginings of many years, weakness and self-doubt. Within the context of the weekend, though they may not have been explicit, I was empowered to revisit the dark side of me with courage and a sense of support that though unspoken, was sufficiently strong. I believe this to be true for others too. If only in that respect, despite the system, then the opportunity for learners to achieve a proper sense of self worth is at least the building block for mental and social health and for that learning which we all seek . . . I am still questioning.

Chapter 5

The Story of the Silent Woman: Reflections on Power

Our view of man will remain superficial so long as we fail to go back to that origin, so long as we fail to find, beneath the chatter of words, the primordial silence, and as long as we do not describe the action which breaks this silence. (from *Phenomenology of Perception* by M. Merleau-Ponty)

Shifting the Power Relationship

Teachers and their students are inevitably locked into a power relationship. This is as much so for the tutor or trainer of professional adults as it is for the infant school teacher in the classroom with the little ones. This is an uncomfortable and threatening yet inevitable fact. Uncomfortable, because it conflicts with deeply held notions of equality and democracy; threatening, because it opposes the tutor's attempts to share unreservedly with students the triumphs and traumas of learning; inevitable because it reflects the power relationships in society which are deeply embedded in our consciousness.

This relationship of power has been central to the discussion of the last two chapters. In its attempt to transform this relationship, the interpretive model challenges the expectations which participants bring to a course concerning the tutor's power. The enquiring tutor's concern here to shift this power relationship is not only in order to develop a more 'effective' climate for learning, but also as part of a more general project of emancipation from the power structures inherent in all educational and professional settings.[1]

Attempting to work in this way, with its emphasis upon negotiation and personal reflection, often creates anxiety both for the tutor and the students. As the case study of the previous chapter indicated, this anxiety is initially felt by the students as an awareness that they are not receiving the direction they expect and feel they need. For the tutor, it is felt as an anxiety about being cast, by them, in the role of 'director' of their learning while at the same time feeling that they will not appreciate the value of having responsibility for their own learning placed upon them.

The interface between the students' anxieties and the tutor's can be fraught with tension and even anger. This tension needs to be acknowledged if control is to be redistributed and a more genuinely collaborative environment is to emerge. Only then will participants feel free to communicate openly and have an influence upon decision-making. These are necessary prerequisites if participants are to make use of a group in order to reflect critically upon their own professional practice in ways which take account of their own interests.

My purpose in this chapter is to examine more closely how shifts in this power relationship are experienced. What exactly prompts these changes? What is the nature of the tension and how is it resolved? What is the role of reflection in this process? And what can the tutor do to promote these changes?

The Significance of Silence

In order to explore the power relationships amongst the participants on a course, and how these relationships move (hopefully towards a more collaborative stance), the language used in the group settings is obviously going to be an important factor. What is said at those moments of tension or insight when the dynamics of the group appear to shift, is of particular interest. From my notes and discussions with participants, however, what has become significant for me is not so much the utterances as the spaces between the utterances at these key moments. Just as in the construction of a piece of music, or of a sculpture, it is the spaces as much as the material which carries the meaning of the work, so, in the dynamics of a group's interaction, it is the spaces between words which carry much of the significance. Silence carries with it a wide variety of meanings.

During moments or periods of silence in a group's interaction, it appears that people become more conscious of the process that is taking place. For example, a pause in a conversation in which I am taking part makes me aware of my own role, and possibly the role of others. My immersion in the talk itself is suspended as I become aware of how I am interacting with the others, how others are interacting with me and with each other. What had, a moment ago, been experienced from the inside is now experienced from the outside. The tide of the conversation which had held me, has now left me high and dry. How is the contact to be regained? At times like this thoughts and feelings arise which may be difficult to express but which gain an intensity as the silence continues. Or I may find myself thinking about myself or others in the group in ways which I would not be prepared to reveal. As the length of the silence increases, so greater significance is placed upon what is said next, and so the risk of saying anything increases, threatening to extend the silence still further.

While such silences may indicate important shifts in the way the participants work together, they often provoke anxiety. Typically, tutors only tolerate the shortest of silences in seminars and group discussions. By filling silences with more directions and questions, they may well be imposing their own agenda inappropriately upon their students. But, more specifically here, filling silences may be a way of avoiding the kind of situations in which they feel their confidence crumbling and their own power role becoming problematic.

On courses which aim to make some shift in the power relationships, it is important therefore to resist the temptation to fill silences. Rather than see silence as indicating a problem to be avoided, or even as a weapon of resistance (see Rudduck, 1978) in the hands of the students, perhaps silence could be valued as a way of introducing a reflective space in the interaction. Indeed, the preparedness of a group to entertain silence may be an indication of its achievement as an 'ideal speech' community (Habermas, 1974). The freedom to speak entails the freedom to remain silent. But the meaning of silence may be much more than simply the absence of speech.

Introducing the Story

In order to explore the nature of silence in a group setting, and in particular its relationship to issues of power, I shall present a story. The reasons for presenting this exploration in a fictional form are suggested in Chapter 1. The story, constructed using a range of research material, concerns two central characters. Gerald, the tutor, runs courses, mainly for experienced teachers, on teaching methods. Nicola, one of the participants, is a woman who appears to contribute little to the course which Gerald is leading, preferring to remain silent. What does her silence mean? As Gerald, Nicola and the other participants in the group interact during the short course, the story suggests how the power relationships change in often unexpected ways.

Like any novel, there is a sense in which this story is auto-biographical: the author identifies in some way with all of the characters, but is not committed to a total identification with any of them. For example, Gerald, the course tutor in the story, shares with me a concern to run a course in which the participants are led to question the power relationships involved in their professional practice. In this respect, Gerald and I are concerned with the same question. The appropriateness of his actions, however, is brought into question by the story's narrator, who offers another layer of interpretation to the unfolding events; while through Nicola, 'the silent woman' who gives the story its title, yet another perspective is offered as she struggles to come to terms with the course.

I have written the story in the second person in order to give the impression of an internal dialogue which takes place as Gerald reflects on the unfolding events. These reflections offer no solution to the dilemmas they raise, but invite the reader to engage in what seem to be some central ironies concerning the ways in which power is manifested and transformed through interaction.

The setting for our story is a three-day residential course at which Gerald, the course tutor, works with a group of ten experienced teachers to explore new approaches to teaching and learning. The course is structured around a series of activities between which there are meetings when the group reflects upon the last activity and plans the next one. It is during these reflective sessions that moments, or 'episodes', of silence arise. The story is structured around these episodes.

The story opens on the first day of the course. During the first two sessions the participants have introduced themselves and talked about their teaching. Apart from a brief introduction of herself, Nicola has said very little during the sessions.

Gerald has just asked the group to say how they feel about the last session.

The story is taken up by the narrator, who addresses Gerald . . .

The Silent Woman

EPISODE 1

You can't see what Nicola's thinking, can you, Gerald? But you watch her. You're a careful observer.

See the silence closing around her, keeping her in a bubble. She can't break through the bubble. She doesn't want to. She doesn't dare to go outside into the cold and show herself to the others. And anyway, her thoughts are different from theirs . . . off their track. She doesn't understand what they're saying. She's warm where she is — but it's cold out there amongst the group. She thinks she'll stay put.

The silence has lasted about two minutes. Throughout, Nicola sits with her arms folded, looking down into her lap. As during the earlier session, her eyes avoid direct contact with anyone else.

'Come on, Nicola', you're thinking. You wish she had the confidence to say something. Doesn't anyone have anything to say? You're on the spot now. Are you going to help them to say something? You'll have to, if no one answers your question soon. You think you should perhaps have phrased this first question of the session less openly. Has anyone got something to say which you can help them with, or are they all completely at a loss? You feel as though you'll have to catch the ball you've thrown, but wish someone else would catch it. You give them just a bit longer before you might try again to start things off.

In an informal conversation with you after the session, Nicola tells you that she has said little because really everyone else in the group knows much more about teaching than her. They've taught for longer. She says she's not very good at putting her feelings into words, and anyway much of what has been said in the earlier sessions is all too 'theoretical' for her.

Oh I see, Gerald. So you think that Nicola's silence is just a matter of lack of confidence. Well it could be, but there are other possibilities. The silence doesn't unduly disturb her, does it? She doesn't feel responsible for the lack of talk. It's not really *her* conversation anyway. She feels she can't relate to its form and therefore cannot contribute. She does not, as yet, identify with the group and, on the experience of the sessions so far, doesn't expect to take on a more involved role. But to say that her lack of involvement results from a lack of confidence is to account for her behaviour in terms of what you see as her personal weakness.

But you don't feel responsible for this silence you created either; or rather, you don't want to.

You wish the group would take hold of the discussion, but until they do, you feel that it's your duty to facilitate the interaction. By allowing the silence to last for two minutes you are indicating to the group that you are not just going to fill in the gap with your own ideas. This is not like a play where the actor has simply forgotten his lines. But nor can the tutor wait in silence without some anxiety. No, you are enmeshed in a fundamental contradiction. On the one hand you are concerned not to lead the discussion but, on the other, you feel ultimately responsible for its progress.

Clearly power at this point, is located in you, Gerald, rather than in your student, Nicola. You're concerned to make this power relationship one of greater equality, and your strategy of allowing the silence is geared to that end. Nicola, however, does not look for nor expect any change in her relatively passive role. Until she wants some change in this respect, it's difficult to see how you can make the change, at least as far as Nicola is concerned.

The relationship between yourself and Nicola is stuck. There is a danger that she will gain little from the course. You feel that she needs help in directing her thoughts, but are afraid that for you to help her will merely serve to increase her reliance upon you. Also there are the other participants to consider. Some of them (at least the one who did eventually open the conversation) are probably more prepared to contribute than Nicola, and it would be a pity if you, by offering more guidance to Nicola, were to pre-empt the opportunity for others to take responsibility by initiating things.

There is a risk that if Nicola continues to feel outside the group, she will start to become bored. And boredom is a strong defence against any useful learning. Before she reaches that boredom threshold she needs some impulse to contribute.

Is it your job as 'facilitator' to provide that? Or isn't that a role which you want all the participants to engage in? How are the group members going to learn to help each other if they only experience you, the tutor, as providing this supporting function? On the other hand how are the participants going to learn how to support one another unless you provide some kind of model for how such support might be given? This is your dilemma, Gerald.

As yet, Nicola doesn't see things this way. For her this is merely a course which, she is beginning to expect, might be rather boring. And if it is, then she is likely to hold you responsible.

EPISODE 2

We have moved on to the second day of your residential course. You kept the first day fairly tightly to the programme of workshops and discussions.

Nicola continued to make very little verbal contribution to these. After the sessions, however, during the evening in the bar, you noticed that she played an active part in some very animated games with some of the younger teachers, while you spent much of the evening in a quiet corner of the bar with Sue. You seemed to be in deep discussion with her.

It has been decided that, for this first session of the second day, the group would plan the morning's workshop. After announcing some changes in the arrangements for meals, you asked the group if they would like to work on any of the themes encountered during the previous day. A man and a woman made quite different suggestions, after which the conversation ended.

The group has now been silent for about three minutes.

Nicola sits with her fingers tightly clenched in her hands. Her gaze alternates between her lap and the ceiling. She unknots her hands in order to rub the back of her neck, crosses her legs tightly, and then folds her arms across her chest. For an instant she makes a scowling glance towards you. You shuffle in your chair.

Nicola's gaze returns to her lap as angry thoughts flash through her mind.

That bloody man! What does this Gerald man expect me to do, anyway? I can't stand this. I could be working with my children in the classroom, and here I am just doing nothing. Why doesn't he tell us what it's all about? He earns twice as much as me, thinks he's so clever, and does bloody nothing. I'm going to leave after lunch. Oh shit, I can't. I feel pinned down on this chair. This is bloody stupid this course. Why doesn't somebody tell him. If someone doesn't say something soon I'll explode. God, I wish I didn't have such a headache.

As the silence continues you're not aware of Nicola's anger, are you, Gerald? Too deep in your own thoughts. Those old feelings of panic rising. You liked those ideas the other teachers started off with.

But why doesn't someone else support them or give their views, you wonder. You wish Nicola or some of the others were equally forthcoming . . . You feel them wanting you to make a decision now . . . to say something. No, you're not going to . . . Not yet anyhow . . . Oh God, you can feel the pressure of them wanting you to decide . . . try to persuade yourself it's their problem, not yours.

You notice a glance from Nicola. Was that anger in her face? You just look at the floor. Perhaps then they'll forget you exist. Then they'll just have to solve the problem for themselves, won't they? You wish you could just disappear. You can feel them blaming you. Oh God, why do I run this kind of course, you think, wishing you could just give lectures in physics instead.

It is another five minutes, but feels to you like an hour, before the silence is broken by Bill. He turns to face you directly.

'Now look here, Gerald, what are we going to do? We have two good suggestions and I'm game for either, but what I can't stand is all this indecisiveness. Let's have some action. Unless you can get things together you're failing in your responsibilities as course tutor. We either do one thing or the other, or else I'm going.'

Hold it steady, Gerald.

Another moment's pause.

Sue looks around the group, then straight at Bill:

'I don't see why the tutor's got to decide. It's up to us. That's the whole point.'

A somewhat angry interchange of views ensues between the participants about how decisions should be made in the group.

You just look steadily at your feet.

Gradually, the conversation focuses upon the planning of the workshop and you begin to join in.

A lot's happened since that awful session yesterday. The fun Nicola had in the bar during the evening suggests that she feels at ease with the group when they are not in session. But you didn't join in. So while she probably feels part of the group, she doesn't really see you as one of them: for her, you are still just 'the tutor'. Yes, that was a look of anger she flashed at you during the silence. She holds you responsible. Perhaps you feel that's a bit negative, but it does indicate her increased engagement with the group and with what's happening. Part of her would like to leave, but she knows she can't. She's locked into a situation from which she can't simply run away. Her headache is probably caused by nervous tension (although quite possibly aided by a hangover from last night's antics) and reflects the tension between the opposing feelings of wanting to leave and to overcome the situation. While she feels no more responsible for the situation than she did yesterday, it now causes her anxiety: it does matter to her.

Until the silence is broken, Nicola doesn't question her assumptions about your role as the one who is responsible for the learning activity of the course. Although she did not join in the argument about decision making which took place after the silence she has, perhaps, been made aware by the way Bill attacked you, and by Sue's reply, that not everyone shares her assumptions regarding your responsibility.

That it should be Bill — a male headteacher with power and status — who expresses the kind of anger she is feeling, may come to seem contradictory to her. But the irony for you, Gerald, is this: you wish to share your power with Nicola (and others in the group), but you can't offer her any such affirmation of her feelings by virtue of the status which the group inevitably affords you.

Like Nicola, you also felt more agitated during this silence than in the earlier one. That angry glance from Nicola, which you only just caught, focused the pressure and blame which you sensed the group was putting upon you. You cannot return the anger which you sense, for that would contradict your view of yourself as a supportive tutor. Nor do you want to make a decision about the workshop, for that would confirm you in a role from which you are intent upon escaping. Your wish to disappear is even greater than Nicola's desire to leave, for, unlike Nicola, you feel you have brought the situation upon yourself: 'Why do I run this kind of course?' you say.

I suppose the angry exchange which followed the silence is likely to have cleared the air a bit. You must feel grateful to Sue for supporting you against Bill's aggressive intervention. While your choice not to join Nicola and the others in their games at the bar last night might have put a distance between you and many in the group, the relationship you have established with Sue seems to have proved crucial for you.

At the time, you must have felt hurt by Bill's criticism, for his values seem to be not only hostile to you personally, but totally in conflict with your understanding of learning relationships. Nevertheless, you must remember that it was Bill who brought to the surface this issue of responsibility. He was the initiator of a series of exchanges which appeared to change the group's dynamic, enabling it to return to deal with the decisions in question in such a way that you could join in. It also led to your role being questioned. This is a vital stage if the course is to achieve your aim. For this you should be grateful to the headteacher.

But I doubt if that's how you feel right now.

EPISODE 3

Following the silence and the angry exchanges this morning the group had decided to split into two workshops, one of which was to tackle a practical activity with one participant chosen to act in the role of leader, the other to tackle the same task without any explicit leadership. You had chosen to join the group which was to be led by the headteacher, Bill. Nicola had also chosen to be in this group, but Sue had insisted on joining the leaderless group. The workshops finished their tasks before lunchtime.

With the lunch break now over the whole group have got together to compare their experiences of the workshops. In the initial discussion they soon reach agreement that the group with the leader has produced the best results. You attempt to sum up their feelings.

'So we're all agreed, are we, that Bill's group produced the best bit of work?'

Bill smiles broadly at this, glances around the room, and replies: 'Well then. We've cracked it!'

The smile on Bill's face lasts for a few moments, but as the pause lengthens into a silence, it slowly evaporates.

You look around the circle at each member of the group in turn. Sue, sitting on the edge of her chair, returns your glance with half a smile, then looks up at the ceiling and shrugs her shoulders. Nicola remains gazing into her lap, but occasionally peers through her fringe at others in the group.

The silence begins to press upon her. She feels trapped. She has to say something. Someone must say something. The tension mounts. The longer we wait, the more significant will be what is said. Has she got anything significant to say? Yes. No, she hasn't. She feels she should say something. But what? How can she say it? 'Won't someone else say something?' she silently pleads. She is not heard.

As the silence lengthens, several of those who had been in the 'leaderless' workshop exchange glances between each other, but especially with Sue. Bill, meanwhile, keeps his eyes fixed on a point opposite him about two feet above Sue's head. Your attention is on Bill. You don't take your eyes off him.

Typical headteacher, is how you see Bill. In that workshop you felt like you were a member of staff at his school, being told what to think and what to do all the time. You wish the other group would say something about their experience.

Come on Sue!

You're sure they're thinking something which they haven't said. What do you do if no one challenges this idea that Bill's group was best? You wish Sue would speak up. Surely she won't let him get away with this.

Sitting next to Bill is Peter. In the initial session Peter described himself as a humanities teacher with four years experience.

He hasn't contributed much to the full group discussions so far, but when he has spoken, it was in a soft voice and others in the group appear to listen to what he has to say. He was in Bill's group during the workshop, but now looks uncomfortable sitting next to him. His shoulders are hunched, his arms and legs crossed, as he perches on the edge of his chair furthest away from Bill. He looks steadily at Nicola who, for a second, returns his glance. With a slight cough, he speaks.

'Well, our group might have produced the best bit of work, but it was really all Bill's. My ideas never got taken seriously. And no one even asked Nicola how she wanted it done.'

As soon as he stops speaking Nicola directs a flushed smile at Peter. This is the first time she has smiled during the sessions.

Sue then starts to speak about how the 'process' that the leaderless group have been involved in is more important than the 'product'.

'At least we all contributed. We were all involved, even if we didn't finish the job'.

There follows a general conversation around this issue, with Bill insisting that 'if a job's worth doing it's worth doing well. And if it's to be done well, you need someone to pull things together.'

Typical manager, wouldn't you say, Gerald? Yes, you would.

But what about Nicola? Where's she in all this? Her state of tension during the silence was quite different from how she felt this morning. This time she was not blaming you. She felt trapped by the silence and wished someone else would break it, but this time felt that *she* ought to contribute. She felt some responsibility for the silence, but finds this responsibility almost impossible to bear. There is a suggestion that she did in fact have something to say but could not put it into words. From the exchange of glances between her and Peter, and her smile following his revelation, it seems that what Peter said struck a chord with her. He had spoken partly on her behalf, and that no doubt led Nicola to feel that she wanted to confirm what Peter had said. But she doesn't need to say this out loud to the group. A smile to Peter is sufficient.

Nicola may have identified herself with Bill's anger in the previous episode but now, after her experience of his leadership in the workshop, she is glad that Peter has expressed another point of view. She has just begun to be involved in the issue which is at the centre of your purposes on the course: for the group to question the tutorial/teacher role and take responsibility for their actions as learners.

The quality of that silence was also different for you, Gerald. You still felt considerable responsibility for what was to take place — you worried that no-one would challenge Bill's idea — but there was expectation in your waiting. You hoped Sue would come to the rescue to support your idea that it is not just the product of the workshop which matters, it is the process that went into creating the product. No doubt you resisted making this point yourself because you felt it would be more valuable if this insight emerged from the group. But do you notice how, yet again, you are not open about what you're feelings but you expect others to be open? Your expectation that Sue would speak out was perhaps reinforced by your personal feelings towards her. Yes, I remember your conversation in the bar with her last night. Quite intimate, I would say.

But Bill, well he seems to represent those very educational values against which you are always struggling. Quite possibly this reminds you of your own service as a junior member of a school staff under an authoritarian head teacher. If Sue were now to mount a successful challenge to Bill's authoritarian stance, that would surely be most satisfying for you, wouldn't it?

Whatever the truth of such speculations, it's clear that in this case you no longer feel yourself to be the only person upon whom the development of the group depends. You still feel responsible. But no longer quite central.

You've been wanting a conflict between Sue and Bill, haven't you, Gerald? A bit manipulative, that.

But you've not been considering how others in Bill's group might be feeling. Peter, on the other hand, appears to be more aware of the feelings of others who may have felt oppressed by Bill's didactic leadership. His direct reference to Nicola — 'No one even asked Nicola how she wanted it done' — indicates that he was concerned that others in the group should be valued even if they do not readily speak up.

His claim to speak on her behalf is, however, a two edged form of support. It might affirm, for Nicola, her feelings about Bill's leadership. On the other hand, it might also reinforce your view of Nicola as a person who lacks the confidence to speak for herself. Significantly, this 'support' is offered by a man to a woman. It carries with it a confirmation of male patronization, reinforcing the assumption that the 'passive' female requires the support of the 'active' male.

When Sue spoke about the value of the learning process in the leaderless group, and how this process is more important than the product of the workshop, she was raising an issue which is central to your experiential view of learning. But although her contribution here is vital, you mustn't overlook the value of Bill's actions. For it was his authoritarian style of leadership, and his forceful expression of traditional values, which provided the context for this issue to emerge experientially. Without this context, argument about such values could amount to little more than intellectualization for Nicola and perhaps for others in the group as well. As a result of the experience, however, and the ensuing contributions from Peter and then Sue, she has now quite possibly begun to give some form to her inchoate feelings about the workshop.

Poor Bill. That silence really marked his 'fall from grace'. And you seemed pretty glad to see him knocked down a peg. But while he might well have a tough skin — for those with his style don't seem to be noted for their sensitivity, do they, Gerald? — he's unlikely to have remained quite untouched by the comments of Peter and the ensuing discussion.

You really mustn't let him become marginalized. That would not only remove the opportunity for him to learn, but would exclude from others in the group a valuable resource.

On the other hand, if Bill continues to defend his educational stance, and receives support in this from others, the group could become polarized into 'progressives' and 'traditionalists'. That would just lead to a lack of openness. And then none of you'd get much further.

EPISODE 4

The last session ended at tea-time and the group were then free until the evening meal. While you went off on your own to explore the town, most of the others went for a walk in twos and threes, either down to the shops, or over the hills surrounding the Conference Centre. The late afternoon was bright and windy.

Then over the dinner table they chatted about their time off: Sue showed everyone the red shoes she had bought in the sale; Nicola and Peter talked about the ruined farmhouse they had explored across the fields; and you explained to them the main features of the buildings in the old quarter of the town. Quite an impressive lecture you gave them. But did you notice Bill? Bill ate in silence. His afternoon was spent on his own watching sport on television.

After their meal they browsed over some ideas for workshops which they pinned up around the meeting room, while you positioned the chairs for the session.

Soon they joined you in the circle and sat down ready to start. The remnants of conversation died down.

The clock on the wall now shows eight o'clock. That's not bad, Gerald. Dead on time. All quiet and ready to start.

Bill ruffles through some papers on his lap.

He stares fixedly at one entitled 'Experiential Learning: An Approach to Progressive Practice — by Gerald Hume'. Peter and Nicola share smiles before each return their gaze to the floor in the centre of the circle. Sue lounges back in her chair and, with her legs stretched out in front of her, admires her new red shoes, occasionally taking her eyes off them to cast glances around the group.

You close your eyes, but the faint smile on your face suggests that you're not asleep.

No one speaks. The only sound is the shuffling of Bill's papers. Glancing up from these for an instant, Bill notices that several of the group are looking at him. Slowly, and with precise movements, he gathers together the contents of his lap, places the pile neatly beside his chair, sits back and folds his arms. His lips are pursed and his expression fixed.

The room is quite still.

Nicola relaxes into her chair, occasionally closing her eyes for a moment or two. Peter smiles gently at her. Nicola, however, doesn't seem to notice this, as her eyes remain fixed on the space in the middle of the group. After watching her for half a minute, Peter returns his gaze to the floor, flexing his arms and legs silently. Every now and then Peter returns to glance at Nicola.

She remains quite still, her face relaxed.

For her, the silence is one of listening and waiting. Not anxiously waiting, but openly waiting. The space of her waiting is valuable in itself not as a means to an end — the thing which is waited for — but for the contact it is. She can feel things settling inside herself. Let's just hold it there. There's no hurry.

You are aware that this is the last session of the day. Trying to take this one a bit easy, are you Gerald? Not a bad supper, was it? Sue . . . you wish she had come with you on that walk. And her red shoes . . . you told her you liked them, but are wishing she wouldn't try to attract everyone else's admiration. And you wish Bill would stop pretending to read your piece about experiential learning. Goodness knows what sense he'll make of that, you're thinking. That's better. Now let's just relax for a bit before we look at the work Sue and Donna have brought.

A car draws up against the pavement outside the window. Doors are slammed and the car radio can be heard announcing the latest cricket scores from Lords.

Startled, Bill immediately looks to where the sound is coming from. Others shuffle in their places as if woken from a sleep.

You find yourself speaking: 'Well, Bill, I expect you'd rather be at the cricket match, but the rest of us have got work to do.'

Before Bill can reply, Peter says, 'That's a bit heavy, Gerald. Just because you don't like cricket . . . that's no reason to get at Bill.'

Nicola looks at Peter while he speaks. Several people in the group now have their eyes on you.

You blush, shuffle your chair, sit upright and look away from

Peter. You don't reply to his criticism. Instead you turn to address Sue directly.

'Now Sue, would you like to start things off for us? How about the work you have prepared with Donna?' Your voice is clipped.

Glances are exchanged around the room.

Sue doesn't reply to your request. Nor does she look at you. Your face is taut. She ignores you for another moment, then, addressing the woman sitting opposite you, she says: 'What do you think, Donna? Are we going to start things off?'

Donna and Sue soon have the group's attention.

You're feeling put down, aren't you Gerald? So what's been happening? Let's think through that last few minutes. You felt quite relaxed at the beginning of the session. Then thoughts started to fill up your space: possessive thoughts about Sue (what do you really want from Sue?); and your irritation with Bill.

I really think these things have more to do with your own personal problems than with the educational issues at stake. The walk, the meal and informal conversation may have helped you to forget the tensions of being the tutor on this experiential course. But, freed from this struggle, you really have shown yourself to be extraordinarily insensitive towards Bill. He hardly needs your sarcasm in order to isolate him even further from the group. And when you are chastized for this by Peter, you immediately attempt to divert attention from your own embarrassment by appealing to Sue and Donna to get the session started. But Sue doesn't allow herself to be used by you quite so easily. In refusing to look at you, or reply to you directly, she is asserting her (and Donna's) independence. And this makes you even more embarrassed.

It's significant that you make this dominating move in order to defend your pride whereas, in the previous episodes, you withheld from any directive actions for the sake of your educational values. After the afternoon's relaxation you might feel free from the burden of the tutor's role and thus at liberty to influence the group as an equal. But you're really a bit naive here. Don't you see that your role as tutor is socially constructed? You are the tutor, Gerald, whether you like it or not. While you may have felt more at ease with the group at the beginning of the session, this does not mean that your contributions are not still invested with the authority of the course leader.

And what's all your hostility towards Bill about? Why did you think he was only 'pretending' to read your article? Why should he want to do that? Wouldn't it be more likely that Bill, having begun to feel isolated from the group by the events at the end of the last session, and during the free time, was appealing to your article in the hope of gaining some understanding of what this experiential course might really be all about. He realized from the eyes that were directed towards him that the others didn't like him reading at that point, and so quietly put his papers down. But then to be rebuked by you as a result of a totally chance event — the radio outside the window — must have confused and hurt him still further.

You remember the way Peter responded to your outburst against Bill? He obviously saw it as an outright breach of the group's trust. Then, to regain that feeling of trust, he even jumped to the defence of Bill, whose leadership style in this morning's session had made him feel so angry. The way he rebuked you — 'That's a bit heavy, Gerald . . .' was firm but not bitter. What an assertive way to defend the group's values! And even against you, the very course tutor who is supposed to represent those values. A powerful move, that.

The afternoon break has clearly reduced the tension in this silence for Nicola who has apparently made friends with Peter. She no longer feels that demands are being placed upon her and enjoyed the silence to let things settle.

The exchange of smiles between Nicola and Peter at the beginning confirms their friendship, but Nicola's feelings towards Peter are not ones of dependence. For when, later during the silence, Peter continued to smile and glance towards her, as if to continue the link between them, she was absorbed in the moment. While she values Peter's friendship, she did not need his continued support during the silence.

This is all very ironical for you, isn't it Gerald? For nearly two days now you've been trying, with little success, to shift the power in the group away from you. And now, because of your crass insensitivity towards Bill, the opportunity has arisen, through Peter's criticism of you, for the group to take away your power.

You just can't win. As long as you're in a position of objective authority, you are unable to step down, for the act of giving power is itself an assertion of power. For power to be transferred away from you, it needs to be taken. And that hurts, doesn't it?

Indeed, the irony was compounded by your own futile attempts to regain your authority by directing Sue to introduce the group to its work. If you had succeeded there you would only have gained the very power which you claim you don't want. There is little doubt, though, that you've been removed from your pedestal. You've been shown to be flawed. You'll not be held in awe in future, especially by Nicola.

You have not come down to their level, Gerald. You've been brought down to it. Oh dear!

Now, assuming that you're prepared to reflect on this event and your own embarrassment, you are faced with a dilemma concerning how you should act on future occasions. Either you stick more carefully to your values of mutual respect and responsibility, and thereby remain in a position of power as the guardian of those values, or else you allow yourself to fall from grace in order that the other participants can take on that role. But such a fall cannot, in good faith, be engineered. How, then, can you achieve your educational objectives? This is all beginning to feel a bit manipulative to me.

EPISODE 5

It is now the second session on Sunday morning and the closing meeting of the course.

The Saturday evening session didn't end until ten o'clock, after which you all went down to the bar and talked in twos and threes for an hour or so. Then Peter, Nicola and Bill left together, while Sue suggested some amusing games to those of you who remained. Do you remember sitting next to Sue and joining in? You didn't say much. Sue seemed to be leading the joking and laughter.

Over breakfast in the morning, after Bill walked into the dining room limping, Nicola told everyone how, at midnight last night, she and Peter and Bill went for a walk up to the stone circle on the moor. Being midsummer's night, they had dared each other to go up there to celebrate the solstice. Once there, poor Bill fell over one of the stones and Peter and Nicola almost carried him back to the Conference Centre with a sprained ankle.

During the first morning session the group prepared some ideas to use with their children back at school. On the programme for this final session was a course review. For this, you prepared a brief open-ended questionnaire which everyone filled in during the first quarter-of-an-hour of the session.

You have now just gathered the group together again and the conversation soon dies down. It seems that the group have got used to starting their meeting together with a moment or two of quiet. There is a certain ease in the way everyone relaxes into their chairs.

Peter grins at Bill's bandaged ankle and then winks at him. You look at Sue and, when she smiles at you, immediately return the smile for an instant before settling your eyes on the floor in the middle of the circle. Bill eases his leg into a more comfortable position.

You start off the session.

'I wonder if anyone has anything to say about what the course has meant for them?'

There's a pause. You continue, hesitating.

'Well I . . . I think I've learnt a lot . . . It's about working with people. Yes. But I don't know. I think I need a bit longer to think about it.'

While you are speaking, several people look at you.

Nicola inclines her head slightly and says 'Mm', keeping her eyes on you for a moment longer. She then relaxes her face and seems to be gazing at a very distant point. Or perhaps beyond it. There is no sign of movement or tension in her body: no itch or ache, no struggle or worry, not even a thought, to separate her from the others.

Then slowly, as if from nowhere, some words come to her: Silence is communion, being held and holding, contact beyond words. She stays with her words.

You haven't yet found Nicola's quietness, have you Gerald? But you're getting there. You're thinking that what you said sounded vague. Yes it did, but you can't put into words what you have got out of this. It just feels better. Yes, you can say what you want, but you feel you don't have to say anything. Even Nicola can be silent. But she needn't. You know. You all know. Know what?

Nothing . . . Nothing. Nothing seems a good place to start from. A clear ground to build on. Now we could start to learn something together, you're thinking. This end could be the beginning. But for the moment . . . nothing.

Within the circle there is no movement.

Through the open window comes the sound of distant footsteps. There is an occasional clank of bottles and the intermittent whir of a milk float progressing down the street. A breeze slightly shifts the velvet curtain by the window, and brings with it a smell of Sunday cooking.

Six minutes after you had spoken Nicola, without moving her body says, 'It's Monday tomorrow.'

So that's it, Gerald. What more is there to be said? She can't answer your question about what she's learned. And nor can you. (Can you ever?) But you can see what's happened. Did you notice how easily she broke that silence? Speaking to the group after six minutes of silence is an assertive act. No struggle, no great intellectual con-tortions; just a simple expression of ending. And now that's taken the group out of its silence. People are seriously, but lightly, talking about the weekend: how strange it has been; how uncertain about whether they've enjoyed it or hated it; a feeling here that it has been significant, but an unsureness about why. Something to be learnt from rather than a content to be learnt. Even Bill — with his sprained ankle which Nicola and Peter looked after last night — looks somehow softer. You can see someone there who's not just a headteacher.

But it's a pity you couldn't see inside Nicola during that silence before she spoke, or during that session yesterday evening. Perhaps then you would question your assumption that her quietness is that of someone who lacks confidence. Would you have jumped to that conclusion if she had been a man, I wonder?

Whether or not she learns something from this change which can be applied to her own work with people remains to be seen. But she will at least have experienced a context for her learning which offers an alternative to the power relations which she is used to at work. It is a context in which her qualities of reflectiveness, quietness and openness to others are given value in her struggle for personal responsibility. While this experience may not be a sufficient condition, it may be an important one if she is to reexamine the dynamics of her own professional relationships.

And what about you, Gerald? You felt this silence quite differently from the earlier ones, didn't you? Having asked the group to consider what they have learned, you then offered your own tentative response. Not like the earlier sessions where you always left them to answer the difficult questions. You no longer felt that your contribution would unduly dominate the group. Perhaps you're right there. For just as you expressed yourself with uncertainty so you put no pressure on them to speak. You were no longer obsessed by the burden of your role. Nor were you wrapped up in your concerns and insensitive to others like you were yesterday. Your freedom to be tentative, to expose your uncertainty, and to stay with the stillness which ensued, was the result of the same kind of changes that have enabled Nicola.

Like Nicola, what you learn from this experience will depend upon how you reflect upon it. Your preconceived notion of her as lacking confidence needs reexamination if you're going to avoid reinforcing sexual stereotypes in future. You also need, perhaps, to reconsider the value of silence as an individual's contribution to a group: is the silence of a participant necessarily to be seen as a 'problem' to be overcome?

No doubt you'll think about the changes in the relationships within the group during the course. You may feel that your objectives in terms of the distribution of power in the group have been met, but to what extent has this been the result of your intentions and skill? And crucially, how will you face the central irony of your position: that you cannot give power to your students? They must take it.

Notes

1   In this respect the enquiring tutor shares the action researcher's purpose, although it must be recognized that such emancipation can only ever be partial. This point is discussed in detail in Carr and Kemmis (1986) chapters 7 and 8, pp. 179–224.
2   See also Rowland (1991a) pp. 95–111, in which the story told in this chapter was first published and the background to it is presented in more detail.

Chapter 6

In the Eye of Understanding

The understanding, like the eye, whilst it makes us see and perceive all other things, takes no notice of itself; and it requires art and pains to set it at a distance and make it its own object. But whatever be the difficulties that lie in the way of this inquiry; whatever it be that keeps us so much in the dark to ourselves; sure am I that all the light we can let in upon our minds, all the acquaintance we can make with our own understandings, will not only be very pleasant, but bring us great advantage, in directing our thoughts in the search for other things. (from the opening paragraph to John Locke's *Essay Concerning Human Understanding*, 1690)

Paying Attention to Experience

Whether or not we learn from our experience depends largely upon how we focus our attention. John Locke reminds us of the difficulty of thinking about our own understanding (or learning). While the problems of the professional to whom this book is addressed may seem less abstract than those of the philosopher, the problem is of the same order: we are often 'much in the dark to ourselves' concerning our understanding of our day to day professional practice. How, then, do we come out of 'the dark', and come to new understandings of our practice?

Diary Entry

Normally, when I do something, I do it because I have some idea of the consequences. I turn the tap and expect the water to flow.

Sometimes when I do something, I have some hope, or I make a judgment concerning the consequences. I reach for your hand and wait for its holding.

At times I express myself without regard for the consequences. In a cry of pain I have no purpose.

But can I act, with full regard for the consequences, but without knowing what to hope for, or what to expect?

As a child, I dropped a stone into the water-butt, expecting it to splash and sink. Expectations were confirmed, hypotheses tested.

The first time I dropped a stone into water, I did not know what to expect. But I had regard. Without that regard I would not have learnt to expect.

My not knowing was the fertile ground for learning.

There was space for coming-to-know.

But sometimes now I have to destroy, for my mind seems to be too full of things known to allow space for the things which are as yet unknown.

The last two chapters have been about creating that space: the context from which new knowledge about ourselves and our work can emerge. If Gerald, Nicola and her friends from the last chapter achieved anything during their time together, it was as much about unlearning or throwing out old ideas as it was about gaining new ones. As they began to face the contradictions underlying their work together, and thereby challenge their expectations and assumptions about the situation and about each other, so they prepared the ground for new understandings.

Although the development of the appropriate relationships for learning is vital, the process of learning together involves more than this. This chapter will move on from these processes and focus more directly upon how they lead to the acquisition of knowledge. In terms of the interpretive model outlined in Chapter 2, the emphasis will now be on the movement between the phase of reflection in which participants identify their needs, and that of provision in which new knowledge meets those needs. 'How does this new knowledge arise?' and 'What is its relationship to experience?' These are the kinds of questions which will be explored here with reference to specific practical features of course work. But first of all, 'What is professional knowledge?'

Professional Knowledge: The Tacit Dimension

While bureaucratic interests in many of the so-called 'caring' professions may challenge us to describe professional knowledge (or skill) in terms of lists of 'competencies', this reductionist approach does not readily provide an adequate account of the abilities we use at work.

It is notoriously difficult to articulate our professional knowledge. If it were not so, my task in writing this book would be no more than a matter of ordering and putting down my knowledge on paper; whereas in fact it is a process of struggle and discovery as I become increasingly acquainted with my own understanding through writing it.

This submerged aspect to professional knowledge is paramount for anyone whose working life involves judgment based upon more than merely technical understanding. We are reminded of it when, in new situations at work, we become aware that we know something we didn't realize we knew, or conversely, that we don't know something that we didn't realize we didn't know. Such awareness is a product of reflection upon the experience: through reflection we can become more acquainted with what we know, what we do not know, and thereby what we need to know.

The philosopher Polanyi used the term 'tacit knowledge' to indicate this submerged nature of knowledge: that knowledge exists at various levels of consciousness. Indeed, he went further, viewing *all* knowledge as being either tacit or else rooted in tacit knowledge (Greene, 1969), in other words, all that we know we are either largely unaware of knowing, or else it has emerged out of knowledge of which we were largely unaware.

A typical example of tacit knowledge is the way I use complex rules of language to speak, while I am unable to explain why I use those rules in that way. On the other hand, the simple rules of grammar of which I am aware, are ones which I was probably able to use effectively before I ever became aware of how I used them. In this way, the simple rules of grammar which I am now able to explain, are very directly 'rooted' in tacit knowledge, while the more complex rules are only tacitly known. Other things that I know (like the date of an historical event) are much less directly rooted in tacit knowledge, but even such things can be traced back to their roots in tacit knowledge, according to Polanyi.

It is interesting to apply this line of reasoning to professional knowledge, particularly that related to the skills involved in working with people. Consider, for example, the dentist who welcomes a patient into her surgery, immediately makes eye contact with him, smiles readily, asks him about his children, and so on. Such procedures are evidence of her skill in putting the patient at ease. The skilful dentist does all this without thinking and may even be largely unable to give an account of the knowledge upon which her actions are based. Her mastery in this sequence is like the mastery of language; it is built upon knowledge which is tacitly held.

Recognizing the importance of the tacit dimension to professional knowledge, the question of professional learning centrally involves the process of reflection. For reflection is necessary in order to bring knowledge tacitly held into a higher state of awareness. Only then can this knowledge become subject to a more critical reappraisal with a view to its development.

Returning to our hypothetical dentist, if she is to develop further her skills of introducing patients, she must reflect upon her experience of introduction in order to raise her awareness concerning the tacit knowledge that she is employing. What then is this process of reflection and how exactly does it change experience?

The Dilemma of Reflection: Whether to Live or Tell Life's Story

Rather than present this problem in theoretical terms, I shall identify it through exploring a specific practical problem: should participants take notes during small group teaching? For underlying this problem, is a much more general dilemma concerning how we can produce knowledge through reflection upon experience.

Note-taking seems to provide an appropriate context for exploring this more general issue of reflection since the students' purpose in taking notes during a session is to help them to gain knowledge by reflecting upon the experience. This is how a student of mine, Adrienne, described her dilemma about taking notes, in a piece she wrote shortly after some working sessions:

> I started to take notes on Saturday because, having written up Friday evening's happenings on Saturday morning I found my memory of events imperfect. However it was a mixed blessing — the open file on my knee was a physical barrier. The act of jotting down a note on one thing meant that I was in danger of missing what was said next. I couldn't expect people to stop while I jotted down their *bons mots*! I tried to keep my writing to a minimum but I think on reflection I entered into things

better when I wasn't taking notes at all. On the other hand I have only a vague impressionistic memory of the discussions after coffee . . . I do not trust myself to recall a full account . . . I have not managed to solve the problem of note-taking satisfactorily in my own mind. To 'experience' most fully it seems necessary not to make notes. To remember most accurately it is necessary for me to make some. With one mental eye on the credit I hope to earn (i.e. the written course assignment) note taking must take precedence . . . I find I need 'word hooks' on which to hang my memories of sequence, exact phrases, logic and emotions. Learning at one remove seems more effective in this circumstance perhaps?

The final question mark suggests Adrienne's remaining uncertainty about this. Her problem is not just the physical one of the time involved in taking notes, but the nature of the orientation to the experience which is demanded by that process. It necessarily leads to 'learning at one remove', as she puts it, as opposed to being able 'to experience most fully' what is happening.

It is fascinating to compare Adrienne's dilemma here with that of Roquentin, the subject of Sartre's novel *Nausea* (1963). The book opens with Roquentin reflecting upon how he is going to learn from the details of living:

The best thing would be to write down everything that happens from day to day. To keep a diary in order to understand. To neglect no nuances or little details, even if they seem unimportant, and above all to classify them. I must say how I see this table, the street, people, my packet of tobacco, since *these* are the things which have changed. I must fix the exact extent and nature of this change.

As the novel develops, Roquentin's view of 'reality' takes on a strange, nauseous, feel as he attempts to carry out this project, being unable to decide whether it is these little things or himself that changes. In the process, he makes a discovery which is rather like Adrienne's (and central to Sartre's philosophy): that life is not a story, it is not an adventure, it does not have meaning in being *lived*, its meaning only arises in the telling of it, from the distance of reflection. One can live or tell; not both at once.[1]

Caught in such a dilemma as this, Adrienne had to judge what was the appropriate orientation for her to have towards the group interaction she was engaged in: was she to 'live directly' with them or 'learn at one remove' from them? This is an issue which I raised with her at our next tutorial session about two weeks after the small group work.

Fieldnote

Adrienne had written a very full account of what had taken place during the sessions. When she came to see me I told her that her account was very useful and had helped me to understand what had taken place. I supposed that she had been able to make such a complete record because she had taken notes. I asked her whether, in retrospect, she now felt this note-taking had been helpful. Was she now glad that she had done it?

'I liked to write up what happened after the sessions. Without notes I found that I could not remember the sequence of the argument. I was just left with a vague impression but unable to recall what actually happened.'

'Did having to write an assignment affect your decision to take notes?' I asked.

'Yes, it did. I felt I had to remember so that I could write it up . . . but I felt more distanced by note-taking. Not so emotionally involved.'

'What if I had taken notes?'

'It would have been seen differently for the tutor to be taking notes. You might have been making judgments about us.'

Should I have made a ruling about whether or not the students should take notes, I wondered. Adrienne didn't think I should have, that it was up to individuals. She took notes, she said, because of her conditioning. One always took notes in lectures. She was modelling her expectations for the course on normal 'lectures', she admitted.

'But there are alternatives which you might model your expectations upon', I suggested: 'Would you have taken notes if, for example, this had been called 'group therapy' rather than an academic course?'

'No, then I wouldn't have. Then I'd have been in a "gut-reaction" mode. It would be the whole person.'

So this seemed to be the crunch. Because this was a 'course' she did not expect to use 'the whole person': it was about remembering things not about emotional engagement. 'Education' seemed, for her, to be about reflection and intellectual activity and, for that reason, not about the 'whole person'.

Like many students, Adrienne models her decision to take notes on her experience of note-taking during 'normal' academic courses of lectures. It is interesting to compare the effectiveness of this strategy with the findings of empirical research. A range of studies have demonstrated the ineffectiveness of note-taking. In one such study (Hartley and Cameron, 1967) students' notes were found to contain, on average, only one in five of the informational units presented. But even more significantly, while students claimed that they took notes in order to help them revise, 87 per cent of these students did not subsequently even read these notes. In general, the evidence of such studies suggests that, even in formal lectures, students would do better to engage wholeheartedly with what is being said than to distance themselves from events by the process of note-taking. In small group work, where the participant has a greater responsibility to contribute, note taking would seem to be even less desirable.

This question of note-taking is only one practical implication of the more general dilemma of reflection: that the state of consciousness demanded by reflection is different from that demanded by engagement with the moment to moment flow of activity. A very different instance of this problem arises for the ballroom dancer teaching a new partner the steps. While he is normally able to dance gracefully enough without thinking of his feet, once his attention is turned to demonstrating the position of the feet, he treads on the toes of his new partner or gets in a tangle. Describing this kind of problem, Polanyi (1961) writes:

> The identification of the constituent motions of a skill tends to paralyse its performance. Only by turning our attention away from the particulars and towards their joint purpose, can we restore to the isolated motions the qualities required for achieving their purpose. (p. 126)

Polanyi's advice to the dancer worrying about his feet, or to Adrienne worrying that she might forget the details of the argument, would be the same: redirect your attention towards the overall purpose of the activity, be it cycling or a seminar.

This attention to overall purposes — or 'going with the flow' — is integrative: it is an orientation to experience which integrates rather than reflects upon the constituent elements of knowledge or skill involved. It is an experiential mode of perception, which is appropriate to the experiential aspects of course work.

But for new knowledge to be realized, an analytic or reflective orientation is required as well as an integrative one. If the discussion so far has suggested that reflection presents us with a dilemma *vis-a-vis* lived experience, that is not to undermine the importance of reflective and analytic ways of being. It does, however, suggest that we need to be clear about the extent to which different aspects of course work might demand an experiential as opposed to an analytic mode of perception.

Analysis and the Emergence of New Understanding

Academic coursework tends to demand an orientation which is reflective and analytic. Most professional courses, however, combine this academic feature with an experiential one in which professional skills are practised and other processes engaged in which may then become the focus of reflection. I now want to consider how students move out of an experiential orientation into a more reflective one in which an analytic orientation is demanded and relationships are made with other sources of knowledge.

To do this, I shall give a very brief account of how three participants on a course, which highlighted group learning, decision making and group dynamics, made use of the experiential aspect of the course in the way they structured the more analytic work which followed on.

Andy, Ivy and Ruth had taken part in an intensive two-day experiential course. Andy was a primary school teacher, Ivy a primary school teacher and Ruth worked as a family counsellor. It was about two weeks later that they each came to see me to talk about how they would make use of the experience in their thinking about their practice. Their meetings with me are recorded in my fieldnotes.

Fieldnote

One aspect of the residential which had most concerned Andy had arisen because I had suggested the participants read an account of the previous year's course before starting on this course. Many of the participants, Andy felt, had been influenced by reading the account of what had been a valuable but intense, personal and, for some, uncomfortable experience. It had, he claimed, made people defend themselves so that they did not take the risks which the previous year's group had. This raised, for him, a very general problem in his teaching: how can teachers share their knowledge in a way which does not pre-empt the learning of the students? This would equally be a problem for the teacher of young children who, in telling a child how to multiply two numbers, prevents the child from discovering the process; or for the therapist who provides the client with an analysis of the situation rather than support the client in framing their own understanding.

In order to explore this problem further, Andy had written a fictional dialogue which he showed me. The dialogue is between a Zen master and student. In it, the Zen master refuses to be drawn into providing the knowledge which the student seeks.

Andy explained how he was very interested in reading about Zen. Among other things, he now felt that it provided insights for him about his practice, and about the kind of things the course had raised, which were valuable. His fiction explored the dilemma with which he had been faced in the experiential setting.

Discussing his account, Andy said that he was currently interested in the idea of exploring writing fictionally. But it would not have occurred to him for a University assignment had I not indicated that such an approach was one that I felt was legitimate. He said that one advantage with this strategy was that it allowed him to explore the issue without having to record in detail the actual events that took place during the residential experience.

He said: 'When you're engaged with how the events happened, you're not engaged with the issues.' He was concerned 'to deal with the issues on a broader plane rather than with the particularities'.

With this approach he did not need, for example, to take notes during our sessions together.

'Not taking notes, it may just be that I'm lazy. But if what happens is significant, then it'll last. Value for me is not in trying to reconstruct what happened but to get further into the issues later by reflecting upon the impressions which the experience has left. Not to analyze what's happening at the time but to experience it — be aware — let it happen to you.'

Fictional writing, he felt, was a way in which he could explore the issues with which the experience had left him. It didn't require him to remember who said what and exactly what happened, but allowed him to build upon the aspects that had struck him most.

He added: 'Then afterwards I look at the issues, the books I've read. Other people's ideas help to clarify the issues.'

I was fascinated by the way he related the awareness of direct experience, his later reflecting upon it, the fictional writing process and the drawing from other literatures. This seemed to combine imagination, exploration and a proper concern for the insights of other people.

By integrating his course experience and his knowledge of Zen teachings through the medium of fictional writing, Andy was able to open up for exploration and critique, the values which underlay his practice. The form of a dialogue was also appropriate since it enabled him to express the two horns of the dilemma he faced: the one concerning the teacher's need to instruct; the other concerning the student's need to discover.

Fictional writing, however, does not come naturally to everybody. Ivy had also been present during my conversation with Andy, but she had found it more difficult to draw upon the experience.

Fieldnote

After we had discussed Andy's writing this morning, we turned to Ivy's. She had written a few pages about her ideas, but didn't seem happy with what she had done. In her writing, she expressed her difficulty like this:

'the experience of the course is very difficult to distil into coherent thought. I have tried listing themes but as in any exploration of an issue, the distilling of thoughts into words can never truly represent these thoughts'

In discussing the piece and her difficulty she said: 'As soon as I write it I argue against what I've written.'

I replied 'Well why not do that?'

I think my comment surprised her. It had seemed to her that her problem was that she couldn't write anything because as soon as she did, she realized that she wanted to say something quite different and often contradicting what she had just said. She seemed to think that 'academic writing' must state clearly positions, demonstrate arguments and so on. For her, it seemed that such writing, of its nature, couldn't be exploratory.

I said I thought that the best academic writing was often dialectical: it expressed and explored contradictory positions and feelings. I thought that it would therefore be quite legitimate for her to write something and then, when she had read what she had written, write an alternative or contrary view which she might also, in part, hold.

We talked about this idea a bit. I didn't have any clear suggestions as to exactly how this might be done. Perhaps she could use what she had already written, select a statement she had made, and just continue to contradict herself and then explore those contradictions.

> *Drawing Andy into the conversation, it seemed that he had liked the approach of writing fictionally because it allowed him to explore the ambiguities in experience. A more academic style, he felt, militated against the exploration of ambiguity. Ivy didn't seem to be attracted to the idea of writing fictionally, but, it seemed, needed another way of writing which liberated her from what she saw as 'academic constraints'.*
>
> *Ivy had started the conversation by saying that she felt the assessment need of producing written work was a constraint on her learning. She felt that she could, if she had to, struggle to jump through the hoop, as she saw it, of producing an essay, but she didn't feel this was the appropriate way to express or explore what she had learnt on the course.*
>
> *As a result of our conversation she went away feeling that there was perhaps another possibility of using writing to get her ideas further. I felt that she would need some support in this and we arranged that we would meet again next term to read and talk about her new attempts to write.*

When Ivy came to see me again she had written an imaginary conversation between two friends. One of these had attended the course and been enthusiastic about its openness and its exploratory nature; the other character had not been there and was highly sceptical of her friend's account, suspecting hidden agendas and manipulation of power. Ivy explained to me how both characters represented aspects of herself. The form of the writing enabled her to explore the value of the experience, but also to express her doubts. This writing could be seen as an attempt to articulate a thesis and an antithesis about power in a small group setting. In this way it represented a dialectical form of enquiry.[2] Alternatively, the writing could be viewed as an articulation of two aspects of her personality which were in conflict concerning these issues. From this point of view the writing represented the feelings of two of her sub-personalities[3] which both demanded to be acknowledged by the multiple self who took part in the experience.

While she did not explicitly draw upon her knowledge from other areas as Andy did, she did devise a way of using writing to explore her, at times, contradictory ideas.

The comments of Andy and Ivy raise serious questions about how students see 'academic writing'. It is not difficult to see where these ideas come from in their experience of institutional education. It is more of a problem to overcome them. It seemed important for both Ivy and Andy to explore ways of writing which could be part of the process of clarification, rather than produce 'academic' writing which, as they saw it, expressed only the product of considered thought.

While Andy's and Ivy's approach to writing as a way of building upon their experience was somewhat innovative, Ruth took a more traditional path.

Fieldnote

As someone who is professionally involved in counselling, Ruth's response to the course appeared to be different from those who were not so familiar with counselling and group work. The processes by which a group negotiates and explores its own dynamics was familiar to her.

So when she came to see me to discuss what she might write as a result of the course, it seemed that she was not so concerned to explore its impact on her personally, but to view the experience in a more detached and analytic manner. She seemed to be at a stage which did not involve personal exploration but wanted to relate the ideas she had gained to the research writing of others.

We discussed a few books and articles she might read. She was interested in looking at different models of learning and group processes, although she said that it was important not to allow one's understanding of these things to be too narrowly fixed by 'models'.

We talked quite a bit about the purpose of models, about the importance of not allowing them to constrain or close off our understanding of phenomena, but rather of giving us a shared language, in an iconic rather than verbal manner, which can help us to consider things further.

What struck me was how different her writing would be from that of others who had not had the same kinds of experience before. She had now clearly identified what she needed in terms of new knowledge. She had formed a range of expectations and skills connected with working in a group. She said that she still worked largely at an intuitive level when she was counselling. I don't think she wanted to stop being intuitive in her professional work, but she did want to develop her understanding further by using other resources.

It is interesting to view what Ruth said here about 'intuition' in the light of the earlier discussion of tacit knowledge. The term 'intuition' has a mysterious ring to it which is demystified by Polanyi's account of tacit understanding. Where Ruth states that she works at an 'intuitive' level while counselling, Polanyi would describe her as drawing upon tacit understandings while focusing her attention upon the 'joint purpose' rather than the 'constituent elements' of her practice.

At this point in the course, however, Ruth took a step back from her intuitive, or integrative, orientation. When she had read from a number of theoretical perspectives she went on to write a critical essay which reviewed these in the light of her professional and course experiences.

At this meeting with Ruth, she clearly reached the 'need for instruction' stage as suggested by the interpretive model. This instruction was provided by the books which she went on to read, rather than by me.

In offering advice about what she might read, I was aware of how different my role had become from that I had played in the earlier part of the course. I was now guiding her towards resources for new knowledge, whereas before I had been a reflective agent within a collaborative setting.

In their different ways, Andy, Ivy and Ruth had been able to transcend the experience they had shared as part of a course which had 'disclosed' for them something of significance about their professional practice. In an article on independent learning, Jourard (1967) describes this crucial point in learning when the learner becomes fascinated:

> Some aspect of the world discloses itself to a person. He 'flips' from the experiential mode of perception (just looking at the world as it discloses itself to him), to an imaginative consciousness. In that mode, he experiences himself as beckoned, challenged, invited or fascinated by this aspect of the world. (p. 85)

Moments such as this mark a most appropriate point for students to turn to resources outside the group now that they have identified their need for new understanding. Principal of these resources is likely to be the professional and research literature which represents the accumulation of the knowledge of others who have explored the territory before.

The Research Literature

When participants enter a course from a range of professional settings, the problem arises of how to ensure that there is an appropriate unifying element to the course. This is often done by giving students a bibliography of readings. Since these would outline the 'field' and perhaps the 'language' of investigation as well as the basic knowledge, everyone should know where they are at the outset, have some idea of where they are going, and a few clues about how to get there.

Such a view, however, is inclined to overlook the personal and creative nature of reading. The meaning of a text for one person is different from its meaning for another. Reading is a process of construction. The way in which a text is constructed by the reader depends upon the context — the history of ideas, recent experiences, professional values, and so on — which inform the reader's reading. We cannot therefore assume that a group of people from a range of professional settings will make the same sense out of a selection of readings.

On courses which include a significant element of direct experience, there is a danger that preliminary readings set up a contradictory set of expectations. On the one hand, the reading list suggests that in order to provide a knowledge base, we can rely upon second-hand experience through reading; but on the other hand the course itself is built upon the idea that direct experience is necessary in order to develop appropriate knowledge.

Such a contradiction readily leads students to experience frustration as they struggle through the 'set texts'. This is how Sue expressed this frustration following a course I had run which involved her in researching her own practice:

> Before the course I attempted to read the two set books on the preliminary reading list but found this a difficult if not impossible task. I reworked my way through parts of the whole but found the emphasis . . . totally alienating. Throughout the course, as well as reading around the area, I persisted with the two books and still had difficulty. Towards the end of the course, when I read the epilogue in (one of the books) I suddenly found it made sense and I had sufficient understanding to receive what was being said. Many of the points echoed my own recent experience and for the first time really made sense. I had needed to share the experience rather than receive it second hand.

The problem here could simply have been that the preliminary texts were badly chosen, or that the research field lacked sufficient definition to make a selection of texts easy. I think, however, that Sue is saying something more significant than that. It concerns the relationship between understanding gained though reading and understanding gained through reflection upon experience. For her it was experience which provided 'sufficient understanding to receive what was being said'. It was where the text 'echoed' experience that Sue could make sense of it. To put this another way, her understanding had to be grounded in experience (drawing upon the tacit dimension of knowledge) and not texts. It was this relationship between text and experience which enabled her to give meaning to the text and thereby illuminate the experience.

A rather different reason for coming to the reading at the later stages of an enquiry-based course were given by Jamie, who had been part of the same group:

> It was only after completing my enquiry that I went to the literature. I would normally have approached the literature at first but I was interested to make my own findings first without relying too much on previous investigations.

While Jamie's approach avoided the struggle which so frustrated Sue, it also reflects a desire for authenticity in his enquiry into his practice. He did later, in fact, go on to consider several texts related to his own investigation, and these enabled him to place his own ideas within a wider context, thus giving added meaning to them. But the step he had taken was as if to say: 'I'm O.K. My ideas have significance. I'll see what others have to say later', a reasonable enough approach for someone who already has considerable professional expertise. It does not reflect arrogance, but a concern to assert the validity of one's own experience. Only upon the basis of this assertion can students begin to engage critically with texts by making continual comparisons between their own experience and what they are reading. As one student put it:

> I don't object to them (i.e. published texts). I just like to formulate my own ideas before I read other people's more 'learned' opinions. Then I know whether the opinions are mine or not.

The ability to make this kind of distinction provides some assurance that the resultant knowledge will be authentic rather than doctrinaire. An attitude of such confidence is particularly admirable at a time when centralized political concerns for accountability have been associated with an increased distrust of the judgments which individual social workers, teachers, nurses and others make in the course of their practice. It is, perhaps, a step in what Polanyi (1958) has called the programme of self-identification:

> I believe that the function of philosophical reflection consists in bringing to light, and affirming as my own, the beliefs implied

in such of my thoughts and practices as I believe to be valid;
that I must aim at discovering what I truly believe in and at
formulating the convictions which I find myself holding; that
I must conquer my self doubt, so as to retain a firm hold on
this programme of self-identification. (p. 267)

There is a danger that more traditional forms of study, in their constant appeal to the authority of published research literature, encourage the very kind of self doubt which Polanyi's philosophical reflection is aimed to conquer. There is nothing like a research text, followed by a long list of bibliographic notes and references, for making the professional person feel like an outsider to the world of academic research. Too many experiences like that can put one off reading professional literature altogether, let alone writing it. The baby is then thrown out with the bath water. Or the alternative danger is that the course participant learns to play an academic game of quoting as many references as possible. The authority of the work is then seen to be based upon the extent of the quoted references, rather than upon the clarity and rigour of the argument.

By the time students enter a course of further professional development, many of them have already learnt to play, and succeeded in, this academic game of 'quoting the authorities'. It is a game which can provide spurious second-hand knowledge which is insufficiently rooted in experience (and the tacit knowledge which is embedded in it) to tackle the real problems of professional practice. Students can find it hard to unlearn this game while retaining a proper respect for, and ability to learn from, the work of those who have 'been in the field' before them.

There is also a somewhat more subtle issue concerning the question of whether students should read after rather than before an experiential course. This next comment from Jeanne, who had taken part in a similar course to Sue and Jamie's, is typical. Here she refers to a book which was on the preliminary reading list:

Had I read this chapter at the start of the course I would probably
have understood where we were heading but not have gained
so much from the process.

The comment was made as part of a course evaluation in which Jeanne emphasized how difficult she had found it to grasp the purpose of her investigations and where they were leading her. It suggests that this feeling of being lost can itself be understood as part of a creative process, once a clear direction has been found. She seems to be suggesting that the process of making sense of an experience which initially appeared to be chaotic, was a valuable one which would have been pre-empted by having read the chapter at the outset.

This is similar to the issue which Andy identified in the earlier part of this chapter. There he felt that reading about the course experience first had actually prevented participants from allowing themselves to enter into the more risky, uncertain and chaotic aspects of investigation and group interaction. Here Jeanne appears to recognize that the working out for herself 'where we were heading' was a valuable part of the learning process.

Throughout this chapter I have emphasized the close relationship between new knowledge and the experience in which it is rooted. These experiences may arise from the experiential (as opposed to the analytic) aspects of the course itself, or from professional practice. Such learning involves the participants in a process of evaluation as they seek to give meaning to these experiences and relate them to the work of others. The next chapter will explore this question of evaluation from the perspective of the course tutor. In other words, how might course tutors gain new knowledge from the evaluation of their own practice of running the course?

Notes

1 For an excellent brief outline of Sartre's philosophy, see Murdoch (1965).
2 For an explanation of dialectics in action research see Winter (1989), pp. 38–68.
3 The notion of sub-personalities and their psychology is explored in Rowan (1990).

Chapter 7

Learning from Evaluation and Assessment

Cecil Graham:	What is a cynic?
Lord Darlington:	A man who knows the price of everything and the value of nothing.
Cecil Graham:	And the sentimentalist, my dear Darlington, is a man who sees an absurd value in everything, and doesn't know the market price of a single thing.

(from *Lady Windermere's Fan* (Act III) by Oscar Wilde)

A Particular Case

Evaluation and assessment are perhaps the most complex fields of educational writing. In their attempts to make sense of assessment, researchers have identified a multitude of different purposes which it can serve[1] and forms which it might take.[2] Writers on educational evaluation have hotly contested the nature of evaluative judgments and the basis upon which they can be made.[3]

Within a field which is so complex, such discussions can easily become remote from the events which they seek to illuminate, by the processes of categorizing and theorizing.

In an attempt to avoid this, I shall start with the concrete and describe a feature which was an element of a specific course evaluation. It is offered not as a model for evaluation but in order to provide a grounding from which to focus directly on how the enquiring tutor can learn from evaluation and assessment and what part the course participants can play in this process.

A colleague runs a one year full-time MSc course for trainee educational psychologists. At the end of the course, he asked me if I would help him by facilitating a student evaluation. He suggested that I might spend an hour or so with the group encouraging them to talk openly, and as a result of this discussion prepare a report. He would not be present at the session.

I know little about educational psychology. I knew even less about the structure and aims of this course, and had rarely taught with this colleague. I was therefore at a loss to know what kinds of questions to ask the students. Although he briefed me, I still felt ignorant. (However much a tutor tells me about their practice, I have little feel for it until we have worked together. Is this feeling of isolation a perennial problem for teachers?)

I nevertheless agreed to the request, and decided to use a strategy which I had found useful in evaluating my own courses. The evaluation meeting with the students is described in my fieldnotes.

Fieldnote

I entered the MSc seminar room at the time we had arranged for the meeting. The students were chatting informally, drinking coffee. The course tutor was not there, though it soon became clear that they had been told about the meeting and that they knew who I was. (I had in fact met the group once earlier in the year.)

We sat in a circle and the nine students told me their names. I introduced myself and explained that their tutor had asked me to help evaluate the course. I told them I knew very little about their work and that the object of the meeting would be for them to give their opinions about the course from which I would write an evaluation report. I explained that in order to do this I would like to structure the session along these lines:

1 *Each student would be given three index cards on which they would have ten minutes to write as follows, without identifying themselves:*
   (a) On the first card: A sentence saying one thing they liked about the course.
   (b) On the second card: A sentence saying an aspect of the course they didn't like, or which could have been improved upon, or a feature they would have liked to have been included in the course.
   (c) On the third card: A sentence making any evaluative comment on the course they chose to make.

> 2 The cards would be placed on a series of tables and the students invited to read all the statements.
> 3 On each card (including their own) they were to score:
>   1 if they strongly agreed with the statement
>   2 if they mildly agreed
>   3 if they mildly disagreed
>   4 if they strongly disagreed
>   or not to make a mark if they felt unable or unwilling to respond.
>   Fifteen minutes would be given to this. Marking anonymous.
> 4 I would gather the cards in and use the statements to structure a discussion in order to illuminate the issues they had raised.
> 5 I would write a report based upon the cards and notes gathered during the discussion.

The students were happy to adopt this procedure and I agreed to let them have a copy of the report.

We set to work. Twenty-seven statements were written and distributed, and the students walked around the tables scoring them. There was little informal conversation over this, and I didn't particularly want to encourage it. At this stage it seemed more important that they give their views individually rather than discuss things.

Once the scoring was complete I gathered the cards together, at the same time sorting them into three general groups: positive evaluations in which there was a general agreement; positive or critical evaluations in which there was considerable disagreement; and critical evaluations in which there was general agreement.

After I read out the positive evaluations which had met with general agreement, the participants expanded on what they liked about the course.

The next group of cards prompted a more lively debate. Some of the differences in opinion related to aspects of the course where the students had actually had a different experience from one another on a work placement. But many of the major differences were between those who would have liked a more 'structured' course in some respects, and those who liked the openness and lack of structure. Some felt the tutor should have been more directive concerning such things as deadlines for coursework, others objected to this view, saying that they 'didn't need spoon feeding'.

The last group of cards — those indicating generally agreed critical evaluations — stimulated a discussion about certain problems which, *it seemed to me, could yield some useful suggestions for future course planning.*

At the end of the session I gave a very brief summary of the impression I had gathered, and the group appeared to agree with this. Finally, I told them I had learnt a lot about their course during the session, thanked them, and left.

A few days later I gave my colleague the evaluation report which I had drawn up as a result of meeting his students. He said that they had told him that they had enjoyed the evaluation session and it had given them a useful opportunity to reflect upon the course.

I also felt the procedure had worked well. It gave what appeared to be a very useful summary of the students' views about what the course had achieved and how it might be further developed.

But evaluation is a critical activity. It involves not only analysis and judgment concerning the object of criticism, but also analyses and judges the process of criticism itself.[4] It is therefore necessary to ask questions concerning the assumptions that underly the approach adopted: What significance can we give to what people say about their own learning? How can the tutor's practice be informed by what students say? What do we mean by success and failure as applied to the course experience? These are the kinds of questions which will now be addressed using the particular case as a point of reference.

Who is to Judge the Value?

So far in this book it has been assumed that the courses we are considering are aimed to meet the professional needs of the participants. Indirectly, courses might also be intended to serve the needs of the participants' clients, their employers, funding and government agencies, and so on. The judgments of such groups of people might therefore be a crucial part of any full course evaluation. With our focus on the enquiring tutor, however, I shall restrict attention to those immediately involved in the course: the tutor and participants.

In the evaluation exercise described above, the procedure was 'student-centred' in two respects: in the usual sense in which the students' views were being sought; and also in the more unusual sense in which they also compiled the statements to which they would then respond.

In the more conventional questionnaire, in which students are invited to respond to set statements or questions, we can never be sure that the questions are relevant to the students. The traditional 'any further comments' section at the end of a questionnaire does little to overcome this problem. The responses to the set questions can be analyzed more readily than the *ad hoc* individual comments, and are therefore likely to feature more prominently in the evaluation report.

In this particular case, one reason for requiring the students to compose their own statements was that I felt insufficiently know-ledgeable about the course to ask appropriate questions. Even when evaluating my own courses, however, I have found that this approach is preferable to the more conventional predetermined questionnaire. By adopting this stance of 'the stranger' (Green, 1973) and allowing the students to define the agenda for evaluation, issues emerge which go beyond what the tutor is able to prespecify at the outset.[5] It may be useful when evaluating one's own course to take part in the exercise (rather than simply 'facilitate' it) and contribute statements on the same basis as the students. This provides some opportunity for the tutor's own concerns to be addressed by the participants without giving them undue prominence.

Underlying this strategy is the assumption that students can give a reliable account of the value they have gained from a course in which they have taken part, and moreover that they are able to identify the appropriate dimensions of such an account.

On the face of it, to assume otherwise would seem to be contrary to the interpretive model. For according to this approach, the students make their own evaluations of their learning directly in terms of the needs they have identified and the extent to which these have been met. But the question remains: how are we to interpret their accounts about the value of their learning experience?

One difficulty here may be a tendency of course participants to indicate positive rather than negative judgments, particularly where the course tutor is conducting the evaluation. In the particular case described, an attempt was made to overcome this problem by inviting a relative outsider to facilitate the evaluation in the absence of the tutor, and by requiring participants to make a critical (or developmental) statement as well as a positive one.

Even if we can overcome such biases, however, and assume that participants are sincere in their responses, the ability of anyone to report on their own learning is still open to question. While we may go along with the humanistic principle that people are the *best* authority con-cerning their own state of mind (Harre and Secord, 1972), when it comes to evaluating one's own learning, more may be at stake than simply 'one's own state of mind'.

The Hedonistic Principle

Hedonism is a philosophy according to which statements about value can be reduced to ones about pleasure or enjoyment. Applied to student evaluations, this principle suggests that students will interpret the statement 'this aspect of the course was valuable' as being equivalent to the statement that 'this aspect of the course was enjoyable'. It is often argued that a danger with student evaluations is that the hedonistic principle will predominate (see, for example, Jarvis, 1983, p. 111). For example, students who are used to a formal lecture format and feel insecure in a less structured setting will tend to find open-ended groupwork less enjoyable; or those who enjoy group interaction will not enjoy the imposed discipline of the lecture format. The danger of the hedonistic principle, it is argued, is that students will emphasize what they enjoyed (or did not enjoy) and that this is not a reliable indicator of value.

In the particular case described above, I asked the students what they 'liked' or 'did not like' about the course, and to state their evaluations in any way they chose. While three of the twenty-seven statements referred to 'enjoyment', most included words like 'value', 'appreciate', and 'benefit', suggesting that 'enjoyment' was not considered to be the sole criterion of value. Those who are impressed by the power of the hedonistic principle might argue, however, that even when students believe that they gained some benefit, this belief may only be in response to their feelings of pleasure or enjoyment.

While it is difficult to provide an adequate criticism of this stance without engaging in ethical philosophy, it is worth noting that if the principle is powerful in relation to students' evaluations, it is presumably also powerful in relation to the tutor's. There is no reason to assume that students are any more hedonistic than their teachers. Both will evaluate from their own perspective, and course evaluation which involves tutor and participants will inevitably be a process of negotiation between diverse subjectivities in which enjoyment is likely to play a part.

Other Factors which Influence Student Evaluations

Opposing the hedonistic principle, however, there is an ethical stance which, put blandly, suggests that 'if it hurts it must be good for you'. On one professional course I attended as a participant I overheard one of the tutors say that the fact that several people on the course had burst into tears at some point was evidence that some useful work was being done! The following student's response in an evaluation, however, is more typical of many on the kind of course which aims at some deep exploration of professional and personal issues:

> I found this course very difficult and not particularly enjoyable, but feel that I have learned a tremendous amount about myself and others. It has made me question not only my assumptions about my professional work, but my assumptions in other areas of life too.

This comment certainly implies a rejection of the hedonistic principle. It may, however, be founded upon the opposing principle which values pain. Before rejecting such an interpretation as being far-fetched, it is worth considering the power which certain psychotherapeutic approaches have had in leading us to believe that learning is likely to be painful (see, for example, the work of Fritz Perls referred to in Chapter 3). If the student has been encouraged to believe that valuable learning is likely to arise out of circumstances which may not be enjoyable, their lack of enjoyment may itself lead them to believe that the experience was valuable.

If such conflicting principles shape the way learners evaluate their learning experience, it is important to ask where they come from. To a large extent this must be the result of prior experiences, particularly within institutionalized education. But also the course itself which is being evaluated will be underpinned by a 'hidden curriculum' which promotes particular values about the nature of learning, and these values are likely to be reflected in the way students evaluate their learning. Some courses celebrate the value of hard graft, with tutors implicitly (and perhaps unconsciously) rewarding students who conform to this value; other celebrate enjoyment, their tutors appearing to be content as long as the participants are enjoying themselves; yet others celebrate painful and disturbing experience as being the path to learning.

Two recent student evaluations of very different courses which I teach have been most striking in this regard. On one of these, the students' positive evaluations were typically couched in terms of the disturbing nature of the experience; on the other, positive values were seen as being the result of hard work and effort. The significance of these student evaluations lay not so much in the extent to which they reflected 'positive' or 'negative' judgments of the course, but that they provided me with feedback concerning the 'hidden curriculum' of the courses. The way in which each course unfolded, and my role as tutor in shaping this, expressed the educational value which inevitably influenced the terms in which the students made their evaluations. This led me to become more aware of these values and the ways in which I was, albeit unconsciously, promoting them during the courses.

Such evaluative material provides tutors with judgments in terms which, to some extent, mirror their own values and aspirations. While this might be viewed as a weakness in terms of their objectivity, its strength lies in the opportunity it affords for tutors to gain awareness of the impact which they have upon their students. Such information is an important ingredient in course review. For this effect to be maximized, however, it is important that students are given the opportunity to evaluate the course in their own terms, so that we might discover the relationship between these and our own aspirations.

Evaluation as a Transitory Process

It is right to give the judgments of students a central place in any course evaluation. Arising from the kind of process described above, however, they are not static 'data' upon which we can base changes in course provision. They are tentative, transitory and open to interpretation and reinterpretation. This is particularly the case in relation to professional courses where an experience is provided which is not part of normal working practice, where support is provided which is not readily available in the work place, and where new challenges are confronted. How a participant feels immediately after a professional course is likely to change once the pressures of the course are replaced by the pressures of normal working life.

A fortnight after a weekend course, David wrote about his experience like this:

> My end of course thoughts are along the lines of: 'the thing which I could imagine as nearest to purgatory would be to have to be exclusively with a group of strangers for a time with no organization and no purpose — I have just been on such an experience and I found it stimulating and instructive — I have learned so much that I am not sure if the world is ready yet for me.'
>
> Well, the problem was not with the world but with me. I feel that I had seen how important people are to each other, how much simple relationships matter, . . . yes I had seen it and experienced it but could not, it seems, absorb it into life.

Result — self appraisal with negative overtones.

Outcome — decided to ignore all that I had learned and get on with life much as it was. This actually has turned out to be impossible because we are the sum of our experiences and the weekend is one which cannot be denied, so I still reflect on the experience, . . . The learning has actually modified my actions and my understanding which is what I think learning is.

Future — I would like to explore more my own feelings but question both the sense of this (would this really be wise — I might not like or know what to do with what I find) and the practicalities (it would require infinite trust). Similarly, I find other people rather more interesting than before but have doubts about pursuing this further. I would not wish to repeat the intensity of the weekend but can learning take place without it?

For what it's worth, that's it. More time to reflect might be useful.

The changes in David's view about the course, and his need for more time to think about it, reminded me of a short course I had attended as a participant some years earlier. Run by a university department, the course had aimed to develop the abilities required to communicate effectively with staff in schools. The course had brought into question a number of personal values about human relations which had been central to my practice of communicating with colleagues. By the end of the course I felt intensely angry, and even wrote to the course organizers to complain that the course had sought to deal with matters which, I then felt, were beyond the scope of professional development. I was disturbed by the kind of interactions that had taken place and felt that highly emotional responses had been unjustifiably provoked amongst the participants.

A year or so later, however, I began to reinterpret my initial response as being a defence against acknowledging things about myself which were vitally important. I had, as it were, resisted learning things which would have involved making greater changes than I was then ready to make. With this altered perspective on the events surrounding the course, I began to realize its value, to work on those changes which now seemed important, and to view the experience as a significant point in my own professional development.

While this may have been an extreme case, the evidence from David's account, and many similar reflections from students, highlights the paradoxical nature of 'success' and 'failure' with regard to course evaluation. Viewed from one point in time, a course can seem to be a failure, but from a different point appears as a success.

In the last chapter, the distinction between reflection and experience was discussed. Indeed, many current models of learning hinge upon a distinction between experience and reflection or between practice and reflection.[6] However, the distinction is not between one kind of phenomenon and another: there are no features which make *this* an experience and *that* a reflection. Rather, the distinction indicates a relationship between two phenomena, the one having a reflective relationship to the other. It is through reflection that experience is given meaning. This relationship holds for courses and course evaluation: the latter is a reflection in relation to the former. Thus course evaluation is a process by which the experience of the course is given meaning, that is, opened up to the possibility of new interpretations.

This accounts for the common observation that participants involved in end-of-course evaluation are quite likely to change their view of the course during the process. It is also one reason why opportunities for formative evaluation during a course are vital, for they enable participants (including the tutor) to gain new insights concerning the significance of the experiences they are evaluating.

When evaluative judgments about a professional course are open to change in this way, it seems trivial to ask students to make a statement about something they liked about the course, or something they thought could be improved upon, as if this were to be the final word. Any course which aims to deal radically with questions of professional practice is likely to leave the participant with a complex set of feelings, memories and experiences which need time to be struggled with and made sense of within changing working contexts. It would be good if we could ask our students to give us feedback immediately after the course, then a month later, then two years later, so that we could really judge the changing impact of the experience. In certain cases, it might be worth overcoming the practical difficulties in order to see how a course can affect an individual in relation to their ongoing professional development. This is a fertile area for further research.

A Longer Term View

In the next extract, Aisha, a social work trainer who had attended the same course as David, wrote about it some two years afterwards. While she had begun to be more articulate about the experience, she was still uncertain about the links between the course and the developing understandings which, she felt, had resulted from it:

A great deal of what happened I did not make sense of then or later and maybe still haven't. It's significance though was the fact that it started off in me the most compulsive search for meaning, thought, and expression that has ever happened to me. It was difficult to encapsulate at all in written forms what was going on for me . . .

It took me a year to write anything about what was, all that time, unfolding . . .

I had what felt to me at times to be real flashes of creativity, making connections, moving my thoughts on. What started for me then has ever since infused great passion and emotion into intellectual enquiry for me both in relation to my own professional practice and in seeking to understand the nature of learning of others . . .

Throughout I became much clearer about how I interacted with others, about what I needed in my learning and how knowledge gained had had profound dislocating, and totally unexpected, outcomes upon my view of myself, my assumptions, and my professional work . . . (I began) to question issues such as the intrinsic structural power imbalances of learning encounters; the power inherent in the position of course providers; the risks inherent in people contracting into learning experiences with unknown consequences . . .

I am still not clear what enabled me to link my experience to this analysis of learning.

Aisha's evaluative comments, written two years after the event, are more stable than those of David written after only two weeks. But for a year she had been unwilling to write, for anyone other than herself, about the things that were 'unfolding' for her and even now she is 'still not clear'. One is left with the impression that, while the experience was apparently very significant for her, she was not sure why or how. Even though she had pursued those issues which the course raised for her into her working life, they had not simply fallen into place. There was still material for her to work on and new interpretations for her to make as she pursues further her 'compulsive search for meaning', which the course triggered, into changing professional contexts.

My purpose in dwelling upon these uncertainties about any learner's ability to evaluate their learning experience, and the transitory nature of these evaluations, is to emphasize the extent to which any end of course evaluation must be provisional. But this is not to diminish its value. Any evaluation can only provide a perspective from a given moment and social location; a perspective from which we and our students can learn and come to develop new understandings of our experience.

Values and Technique

I have emphasized those aspects of learning concerned with personal and professional values and judgment rather than technical features. The mastery of technique (for example, the ability to operate some new information technology, or to get to grips with a new procedure for patient care), and the course provision aimed to achieve this mastery, can more readily be evaluated by the end of the course. Such technical aspects of professional development are important. They are likely to provide a major aspect of course content.

But techniques are always underpinned by professional (and therefore moral) values. Professional judgment is required in order to practise technique in the service of values. While its development is vital, it presents one of the greatest problems in its evaluation, due to the difficulty of bringing it to consciousness.

Professional judgment was at the heart of Aisha's questioning of the power relationships inherent in her role as a course provider in social work training. This area is fraught with values with which she is still grappling, having been stimulated by the course experience. The extent to which, and the ways in which, the course was valuable to her could only be realized at different levels and over differing periods of time.

Some courses fail to address the values which underlie the use of technique. This is because they assume that such values can be accepted without critique, or that questions of value are of no relevance to practice. Such an outlook is technicist: it is an outlook in which 'reflection and morality are displaced to the ivory tower. Thought and wisdom disappear; expertise substitutes itself'.[7]

A technicist outlook in course provision (and hence in evaluation) casts the student as merely a means to a managerial end. It serves to alienate the practice from the person who practises by denying the relevance of moral values. The objectivity that technicism claims to celebrate is bought at the cost of the humanity of those it seeks to control. If course evaluation is to be free of the charge of technicism, it must relinquish such claims to objectivity, acknowledge the subjectivity of the participants, and enquire into the ways in which this subjectivity is shaped by the course and wider social contexts.

It is interesting to reconsider the evaluation exercise described at the beginning of this chapter in the light of these comments. When I reviewed the participants' statements and responses, there appeared to be a distinction between those which related to relatively technical aspects of the course and others which were more firmly rooted in values. Significantly, the aspect of the course about which there was the most marked disagreement amongst the participants related to a highly value-laden issue, namely, the extent to which the educator should 'spoon feed' the learner. This is an area in which we might expect to find these students, as they move into their professional contexts as educational psychologists, reappraising their own practice and consequently reevaluating the course in which they had taken part.

There have been movements towards greater accountability on the part of those who provide courses and an expectation that this should involve participant evaluation. Such an approach is fundamental to the fashionable Total Quality Management system (TQM) which has been characterized as follows:

> A TQM approach is the fostering, throughout the organization, of a process of continuous and never-ending improvement aimed at excellence and customer satisfaction. (Elton and Partington, 1991, p. 10)

Such an approach is admirable and, applied to courses of professional development, would reflect our concern here for ongoing evaluation. There is, however, a danger that in their concern to demonstrate 'customer satisfaction', course providers report evidence of such 'satisfaction' without acknowledging the uncertain and problematic nature of the kinds of judgment involved. Even where techniques are developed to base evaluations securely upon the perceptions of course participants (as was attempted in the example at the beginning of this chapter), they are no more than techniques which must be designed to suit the particular circumstances. The information they produce must be subject to further critical reflection and interpretation if it is to lead to an evaluation from which we can learn. Any attempt to reduce course evaluation to series of ticked boxes and scored statements can be of little value to those who are close to the educational experience, for whom evaluation can be seen as 'a mere beginning in a series of questions'.[8]

Assessing Students' Work: The Contradiction

Course evaluation and student assessment are inextricably linked. Any evaluation of a course must involve, at some stage, an assessment of the work of the students. In this latter, however, the focus shifts to the particular students: their achievements, the quality of their understanding and practice. Whereas course evaluation is readily viewed as a process from which the tutor can learn, student assessment more often casts the tutor in the role of judge *vis-a-vis* the student.

This role of assessor places the enquiring tutor in a contradictory position. For how can the collaborative relationship of the interpretive model, with its aspirations of equality and democracy, survive a relationship in which the tutor stands as judge and even (on professional award-bearing courses) gatekeeper of the students' professional advancement?

Concerned with the process of democratizing education, Freire (1972) said:

> The *raison d'etre* of liberation education . . . lies in its drive towards reconciliation. Education must begin with the solution of the teacher-student contradiction, by reconciling the poles of the contradiction so that both are simultaneously teachers and students. (p. 46)

The enquiring tutor shares this aim with liberation education, but it is important to acknowledge the power of the contradiction at the point of assessment and accreditation. Whatever strategy is adopted, Freire's 'drive for reconciliation' can never be complete. In the end, we come face-to-face with the social relationships which educational and training institutions determine between the tutor and student. While we must seek to change institutional structures in order to affect lasting change here, it is important to be aware of the compromises we are making when this is impossible.[9]

The contradictory role of the tutor was seen clearly in the case study in Chapter 4. The students were encouraged to decide upon their own criteria for assessing their work, and to make their own judgments according to these criteria. The educational value of such a process is apparent. The institution (represented and symbolized by the tutor), however, had to judge the appropriateness of these assessments before offering credit towards the award. In other words, the assessment had to be assessed, thus undermining the educational value of the original assessment process. For a self-assessment which has to be assessed by someone else is hardly a self-assessment!

Here the interpretive model (like any other model) was limited by the social context in which it operated. It represented an ideal which offered guidance, not a technique to be followed. To have attempted to pursuade the students that they could (individually or collectively) have complete control over their learning and over its assessment would have been to deny the realities of institutional power in which the tutor and participants were enmeshed.

This must not, however, become the sticking point. Alternative forms of assessment (student self-assessment, peer assessment and negotiated assessment) may appear to begin to overcome these problems, for they cast the learners in a position of responsibility concerning their own learning. As far as the diagnostic or formative aspects of assessment are concerned, these alternatives present no problems and are consistent with (and even demanded by) the interpretive model. For this reason, some have argued that assessment for diagnostic feedback should be kept separate from assessment for marks or accreditation (see Boud and Lublin, 1982, pp. 93–9).

Many 'post experience' professional and short courses do not involve accreditation, so the issue does not arise with the same force. Even on courses which are award bearing, course participants will often claim that, in all sincerity, it is not the prospect of certification that is of primary concern to them. They have primarily joined the course, they say, for the professional development which it will afford them. With more experienced participants, the problem is often felt more strongly by the tutor than by themselves. On many such courses, there is an implicit assumption that, so long as the participant genuinely engages with the course and its concerns, questions of success and failure are not really the issue. While the judgments of the tutor may be highly valued as feedback to the participants, these judgments are viewed primarily as a formative part of the process of learning rather than a summative assessment of ability.

As students take on more responsibility for assessing their own learning, they also struggle with this contradiction. The following example is extracted from the introduction to a written assignment submitted for credit towards a Masters Degree. Theresa writes:

> The purpose of this writing is intensely personal. I am writing for myself. I am not writing to meet requirements set by someone else, which provides a structure and framework that in previous writing has allowed me to avoid any real consideration of my own thinking. I am not attempting to fulfil a predetermined aim but more to move, through the writing, from where I am now to some position that will be 'not now'. It is a process that I am in control of, not simply deciding content but also being arbiter. Assessing the work myself removes

another prop which would allow me to avoid complete responsibility for the writing and the learning that takes place as it is written.

Although my intentions and concerns are personal, it is important to me to consider that the writing could be shared. It needs to be written so that it can be understood and discussed as it takes place, and I am also concerned that it would make sense to other members of the group and to people who did not share that experience.

Here Theresa both denies that she is attempting to meet the tutor's requirements, and at the same time submits her writing for the tutor's assessment and accreditation. The tutor's power is thus denied in the very act of its recognition! While, from a positivistic point of view, such contradictory action would appear to be irrational, from the point of view I have taken in this book, she is acknowledging the force of the dilemma rather than viewing it as a *problem* which is open to solution.

Secondly, she recognizes that by writing in this way, she 'removes another prop' and takes full responsibility for the process of writing and the insights it offers. The writing, for her, is not an attempt to impart knowledge to be assessed by others, but a means by which she explores her understanding. According to Judith Guest (1986), this is the project of the creative writer:

Writers do not write to impart knowledge to others; rather they write to inform themselves. (p. xii)

Thirdly, her act of responsibility is not individualistic. Although the writing is 'intensely personal', it is not a private journal which is being submitted. Her sense of audience is clear. She is writing 'so that it can be understood and discussed . . . (by) other members of the group and (by) people who did not share that experience'. Such writing is a social action based upon individual responsibility. It is a process by which she makes the personal public and thereby open to critical engagement.

Writing in this way, and submitting it for assessment, Theresa opens up two dilemmas which are fundamental to assessment. The first concerns the conflict between the principle of individual responsibility in learning and the reality of the institution's power of accreditation. The second relates to the apparent contradiction between the personal nature of learning and the public domain which shapes it and in which it is realized.

Traditionally, assessment practices deny both these dilemmas. They accept the 'every day' assumptions that authority resides in the institution; and that the students' understandings are personal and individual. Starting with these assumptions, traditional practices concern themselves with such concepts as fairness, validity, reliability and effectiveness of student assessment. The question of assessment then becomes a technical one of devising procedures which overcome the problems posed by these concepts. Course tutors do, of course, have to address such practical problems. It is important, however, to recognize that the underlying dilemmas constitute a reality within which we must live, and in which we must make our own judgments in the light of the particular circumstances.

Learning from our Students' Work

The introduction from Theresa's assignment from which the above extract was taken, served the function of orienting the reader to the ensuing work. From my point of view as tutor, its implicit message was clear enough. It was an invitation to share in her thinking, and an acknowledgment that while my response to it might be valued, its purpose was not to please or impress me. Accepting this as the starting point, I could then view the rest of the text as something from which I could learn, something which I could relate to from the shared experience of the course and from my different background, something with which I could engage as if in conversation. I felt free to be critical in the sense of offering alternative perspectives on the matters discussed, but not to be judgmental.

The lucidity with which Theresa expressed this orientation to her writing is perhaps unusual, and was to some extent shaped by the way in which her particular course had addressed issues of power and responsibility in education. Her sentiments, however, are reflected in much of the writings of students who have professional experience. They offer the tutor an opportunity to learn from a background which is often wider than their own. Such learning informs the tutor not only about the course processes, but also about the professional issues which inform its content. In this way tutors can learn from their students in ways which keep their courses alive to the issues of current professional practice. Student assessment then becomes a source of learning for the enquiring tutor.

Students' prior experience of institutionalized education readily frustrates the development of such an orientation. Only too often courses then return the student to these paternalistic relationships and stifle the sense of responsibility which has developed since then. Instead, we should build upon the participants' professional experience which has prepared them to be more autonomous in their thinking. Only then can we learn from them in the process of assessing and evaluating our work together.

Notes

1   See Bligh, Jaques and Warren Piper (1975) pp. 20–56 where the authors reduce thirty-two different purposes into six groups concerning judgments about students' achievement, predicting their future behaviour, monitoring their progress, motivating them, testing their effectiveness and licensing their professional practice.
2   Gibbs (1989) pp. 11–17, outlines eleven different dimensions of assessment: informal/formal; formative/summative; continuous/terminal; coursework/examinations; process/product; internal/external; convergent/divergent; ideographic/nomothetic; criterion referenced/norm referenced; diagnostic/predictive; what is learnt/what is known.
3   For a useful collection of papers which takes up the debates on evaluation from a qualitative perspective, see Hamilton, Jenkins, King, McDonald and Parlett (1977).
4   This point has often been made by the educational evaluator Elliot Eisner. See, for example, his preface to Willis (1978).
5   The value of this approach to educational evaluation in general is presented in Parlett and Hamilton (1977) chapter 1.
6   See, for example, the place which Kolb gives to reflective observation as described in Gibbs (1988); or the sequential processes of reflection described in Schon (1987).
7   Inglis (1989) 'Managerialism and morality' quoted in Carr (1989) p. 12 where this issue of technicism is discussed in some depth.
8   Maria Burgio, a researcher at the Institute of Study for Older Adults, quoted in Gamson (1984) p. 165.
9   In this respect the enquiring tutor is committed to the perspective of action research as outlined in Carr and Kemmis (1986).

Chapter 8

Where Does This Get Us To?

'Would you tell me, please, which way I ought to go from here?'

'That depends a good deal on where you want to get to', said the Cat.

'Oh I don't much care where . . .' said Alice.

'Then it doesn't matter which way you go', said the Cat.

'. . . so long as I get somewhere', Alice added as an explanation.

'Oh you're sure to do that', said the Cat, 'if you only walk long enough'. (from *Alice's Adventures in Wonderland* by Lewis Carroll)

The Difficulties of Describing a Course

Alice's adventures gave her much to think about, but the Cheshire Cat was going to give her little by way of a map to guide her through a world in which so many everyday assumptions were to be turned upside down. Her questioning spirit and preparedness to look at things from unusual angles are to be admired. But our students deserve a little more by way of an explanation before they commit themselves to a course of professional development which may well challenge some of their deeply held assumptions about their working practice. Unlike Alice, they cannot return from the adventure to a world in which everything is reassuringly in its right place. They have to live with the consequences of their experience, the new insights, uncertainties and demands for change which it provokes.

We need to be able to orient the prospective student to the course and provide some expectations about what is likely to happen and what will be its value before they commit themselves to working with us. Statements of objectives and outcomes may be part of this, but they are not the whole story. Before signing up, participants need some idea of the 'feel' of the course and what they are letting themselves in for. How can we provide this?

This takes us back to the central problem outlined in the introductory chapter: how can we give an account of the elusive educational processes that take place on a professional course? This final chapter considers how we might communicate such an account to prospective students, and suggests how the outcomes or products of such learning might be placed within a framework for understanding professional competence.

It is difficult to describe a learning experience to someone who is yet to embark upon it. In order to understand a learning process, the person needs to be able to understand the terms in which it is described. Once we move beyond general descriptions of content areas and the surface contextual features, such as numbers of participants, contact time and grouping arrangements, however, the terminology used to describe the process itself is imprecise and subjective. For example, a description of a course aimed to introduce participants to art therapy can give little insight into the quality of the experience to anyone who has not already been involved in this kind of learning process. Even a description of an instructional package designed to teach long division would only be fully comprehensible to someone who already understands something of the techniques involved, and thus of limited use to someone who has yet to learn them. Learning must, to some extent, involve an encounter with the unknown.

The kind of programmes we are considering do not, of course, have to be described so fully. Only an outline may be needed. But on professional development courses which involve the exploration of values, conflicts between values and practice, interpersonal relationships, and so on, even this can present quite a problem. The problem is often side-stepped by recourse to jargon: 'A psychodynamic approach will be used to . . .'; 'through direct experience of dealing with conflict . . .'; 'role play exercises will explore . . .'. While such shorthand may be necessary to describe a short course in the odd paragraph available for an advertisement, it often does little more than mystify the reader who has not already experienced the kind of process described.

The problem is compounded on courses which attempt to adopt a negotiative stance in which participants will have the power to affect what happens. For, as Aristotle pointed out, if we know what the future holds in store for us, we cannot change it; and if we can change it, we cannot know it. The power which negotiation attempts to transfer to the students is gained at the cost of uncertainty about where the course will lead.

There is a danger that this element of uncertainty will leave new participants feeling bewildered by a lack of explicit statements about what to expect. A healthy spirit of adventure may then be replaced by feelings of anxiety and lack of control. This is likely to lead to the course becoming undermined by suspicions that the tutor has some 'hidden agenda' which is being used to manipulate the participants.

A further level of complexity is introduced by the 'market place' environment in which courses are advertised. Within a framework in which training institutions compete for a limited number of students, there is pressure to describe courses in ways which induce people to take part. Fashionable terms for describing courses take on a currency which does more to assure potential participants (and their sponsors) that the course is up-to-date with modern trends than to illuminate the experience advertised. Here professional education and training become susceptible to the same distorting influences of marketing which plague other consumer products. Viewed as a consumer product[1] within a 'free market', there is a pressure to describe the course in saleable terms. It can be argued that such 'efficient' advertising induces consumers positively to prefer shoddy to good workmanship in course design as in any other product.[2]

With these problems, it is all the more important for course providers to attempt to describe what they are offering as clearly as possible so that informed judgments can be made before deciding to take part. In the long term, students are bound to benefit by having access to insightful accounts of the kind of learning they might be expected to take part in on professional courses. It can be exasperating to discover that a participant's and the tutor's expectations about a course are totally at odds.

The course described in Chapter 4, for example, was susceptible to all these problems. First, being an optional course on a Masters programme, it had to attract a minimum number of participants, otherwise the institution would not have deemed it economical to run. The 'market' from which the students were drawn was limited, and it had to compete with other courses offered. Secondly, while its title 'Active Learning' indicated the major theme of the course, as I understood it, it was also a trendy 'buzz-word' in education and training professions at the time. It was thus likely to attract participants who were concerned to keep up with modern developments but were perhaps unaware of the contradictory values involved. Thirdly, its extremely negotiative approach meant that the outcomes of the course, and even the pro-cesses involved, could only be tentatively suggested. And finally, being an experience which was likely to be unfamiliar to many of the students, it was difficult to describe the kind of learning I expected in terms which would be readily comprehensible.

The problem here is not peculiar to this course. For any course which attempts to move away from traditional pedagogies, towards a more enquiry-based and interpretive approach, is inevitably faced with a particular obligation to make its practice explicit.

Engaging our Students

This is the background against which the enquiring tutor's research can be used as a means of engaging prospective students with the educational issues of a course. With this audience in mind, the kinds of questions it might address are suggested at many points in this book: What do the participants expect to achieve by taking part? How does the process develop? How do the participants experience the process? What dilemmas and contradictions are encountered? What are the perceived outcomes? and so on. As well as the tutor's own accounts and reflections, the ideas of the participants expressed in their written notes, assignments and during the course meetings are a valuable source.

Some courses have a particular developmental value: perhaps they are open to a new professional group, or relate to an emerging set of professional issues. In such cases it is particularly useful to write a reflective account, based on this kind of material, which attempts to open up to prospective students the experience of the course from the perspectives of the tutor and past participants. It seeks to evaluate it from an exploration of the issues which emerge rather than from prespecified objectives. It is more concerned to view the course as a case to be studied than to make judgments about its effectiveness.

Such a case study, in the form of a course booklet, provides an interesting resource for prospective participants on further courses of the same kind. They may be able to see their own professional concerns reflected in the experience of previous participants, and gain some insight into how others have grappled with them. They may come to understand the kind of expectations which may be made of them during the course and the kind of commitments that might be involved. While even such a full account cannot overcome the paradox suggested above — that we can never give an altogether comprehensible account of learning to those who have not themselves embarked upon a similar experience — it can at least begin to open up the area. It can bring the course to life in a way that is not possible merely through statements of aims, objectives and methods.

The way in which we introduce prospective students to such a case study does, however, need to be handled with care. There will be a natural tendency for new students to see the course booklet as being somehow prescriptive. So often students are given course guides which detail the content to be covered and books to read at the beginning of a course with the implication that the material to be read forms a basis to the course. While it might inform their expectations, it might also limit those expectations by giving them the impression that their course will be determined by the concerns of the earlier group. It is important, therefore, to make clear to prospective students the extent to which the issues pursued in that particular course resulted from the specific interests of that group. Otherwise, they may see their own experience overshadowed by the earlier course described in the booklet.

Often students want to know if their experience, or their performance, matches those of previous groups. The detailed account of an earlier course group can serve to make them feel secure in the knowledge that their particular difficulties or achievements are to be expected. Discovering that others share your professional problems can be heartening. On the other hand, the process of coming to grips with these difficulties is challenging. There is the possibility that new students may even wish to avoid some of the challenges confronted in the course described.

This can be a problem on courses, such as counselling training, which are likely to lead to a particularly intense exploration of personal issues. Understandably, new students might be made to feel apprehensive by an account of a previous student's troubles. Such apprehensiveness can lead to a defensive reaction as the new students try to ensure that they do not also find themselves in a situation in which they might feel vulnerable. On courses of this kind, however, it is right to warn prospective students of the kinds of demanding situations in which they might find themselves. If, after reading such an account, the occasional student realizes that this is not the kind of course they are looking for, this should not be seen as a failure of the course booklet or of the prospective student. It is rather part of an altogether appropriate process by which students and courses are matched to each other. Any account of a course which aims to engage new students must also risk deterring those who do not share its underlying purposes or values.

Hopefully, however, the course booklet will describe a context of growing trust in which such personal issues can be explored, but also in which individuals can maintain the right to protect themselves from unwanted aspects of personal enquiry.[3] It is an opportunity for the course tutor to clarify the ethical stance of the course as providing a balance between challenging participants to explore issues in depth while at the same time providing a secure environment in which the individual's privacy is respected.

Finally, it is important to be aware of questions of confidentiality in putting together an account of this sort. Perhaps the simplest principle here is to involve students as much as possible in the production of any account which may be made available to a wider audience. If it is not practicable to involve them in the writing, at least they should have the opportunity to view and make changes to early drafts of the work.

It may seem that to involve students in this process places unnecessary demands upon their time since it is mainly for the benefit of future participants. It can, however, form an important part of their own reflection upon the experience of the course — a form of evaluation which is so much more significant to them than the normal requirement to fill up evaluation sheets.

The course booklet, then, tells a story of the course.[4] Like a course guide, it attempts to be informative about the course. But unlike the course guide it describes an earlier course rather than prescribes a future one. It can also be a medium through which the course is advertised. But, unlike an advertisement for a consumer product, it is concerned primarily to attract the appropriate participant rather than indiscriminately to attract customers. Above all, it is a research report aiming to illuminate a particular case, rather than provide a spuriously objective knowledge base. It therefore provides an opportunity to go public by inviting the prospective student to engage with the enquiring tutor's understanding of the course and the professional concerns and dilemmas it will address. Being a product of collaboration, it sets the scene for a relationship of collaboration during the course. While opening up the tutor's practice of teaching, it is dependent upon the tutor's commitment to research that practice.

The audience of the enquiring tutor's research is, of course, wider than simply the prospective students. Educational and training journals are important means by which such investigations can be shared with a wider community of teachers in professional development. The products of research, however, are often criticized for being inaccessible or of little interest to the professional people to whom they relate. By envisaging our students as the first audience and as collaborators in our research, we can begin to overcome the divisions between research and practice, and between the teacher and the taught. It is these divisions which militate against the relationships of teaching and learning which have been the subject of this book. To engage course participants in the enquiry into their own course is a powerful means of reconstructing these relationships.

Outcomes and Competences

Reflecting the general focus of this book, the discussion about making teaching explicit has so far concentrated on the process of learning. However, any attempt to articulate the practice of the enquiring tutor and to share it with a wider audience cannot altogether avoid questions concerning the intended outcomes of a course.

In principle, it is now widely held that course aims, in professional education, as in higher education generally, should state 'what you hope the course will achieve, a statement of what learners should be able to do (or do better) as a result of having worked through the course' (Rowntree, 1986). On the face of it, this would seem to be an altogether reasonable requirement.

On professional development courses, these expected outcomes might be expressed in terms of developing certain professional competences.

The term 'competence' has been increasingly applied to the analysis of professional abilities in health care, social work, education and more widely in the interpersonal professions and in management. Within these contexts 'professional competence' might broadly be defined as the ability to perform an activity which is required in the professional role to an acceptable standard. Thus, for example, a course which aims to develop social workers' abilities to empathize with their clients would be based upon a conception of the role of the social worker in which empathy was a component of competence.

How can such a conception of competence relate to the kinds of teaching and learning processes explored in the previous chapters?

Can the role of a professional be described in terms of competences and how are these competences derived? I shall briefly outline two related problems with this notion and indicate a possible constructive way of approaching the idea of competence which may be helpful in describing the outcomes of the enquiring tutor's work.

The Problem of Reductionism

While any professional person will need to be able to perform certain prespecified activities in order to function adequately in a particular role, the question is: can a professional role be described completely in terms of such a list? If it can, then the problem for describing course outcomes is reduced to one of selecting from the list those competences which the particular course aims to meet. Any other aims would not be relevant to that professional role.

The first problem in deriving such a list would be to decide which competences do not deserve to be included. Knowing how to get to work, for example, is obviously essential for any worker, and a social worker who found it impossible to remember the way would certainly be regarded as incompetent. But such knowledge would hardly be regarded as a mark of competence. It is not an ability which is specific to the role of the social worker. But then neither is empathy. Almost anyone who works with people is likely to be more effective if they are able to empathize with those they encounter. It does seem, however, that a social worker needs to have a particular ability to empathize, often in circumstances in which this is not easy. On this basis it might be argued that this ability is a mark of competence for a social worker whereas knowing the way to work is not.

Let us assume that some such analysis of professional roles could lead to a complete list of competences. We could then imagine a person who had all of these qualities and abilities and could perform all the relevant activities. According to our definition, such a person would be perfectly competent and would thus have nothing more to learn.

The notion of perfect competence is, however, contrary to the idea of the 'reflective practitioner' (Schon, 1987) which underlies so much of the discussion in earlier chapters. For it has been assumed that the effective professional is one who always learns by reflecting upon their practice and is therefore always able to improve. Indeed, the most able professional would more naturally be seen to be the person who is able to learn most from practice, rather than one who has nothing more to learn. The notion of perfect competence is thus reduced to absurdity and together with it the idea that effective practice can be completely reduced to the exercise of professional competences. To describe course outcomes in terms of such a reductionist notion of competences alone would severely limit the possibilities for professional development.

It would be more reasonable to argue, however, that competence is distinct from excellence (or perfection) and that competences relate only to certain minimum requirements. For example, a dentist's ability to drill out and fill a cavity would seem to be a minimum requirement; whereas a detailed knowledge of the latest research in materials used to fill cavities would be above this minimum: one could be a competent (but not, perhaps, excellent) dentist without this knowledge. Making such distinctions, one could envisage a hierarchy of levels of competence, each of which indicates a minimum requirement for functioning to a particular standard.

While it may be easy to distinguish between competences at the extreme ends of such a hierarchical set, it would be quite another matter to define all those relating to a particular professional role and to make a clear distinction between those which are required in order to demonstrate competence at one level from those required at a higher level.

Such a rationale is, however, used extensively in many areas of education and has become a major feature of the National Curriculum and of National Vocational Qualifications (NVQs). In these areas competences and levels of competence (or attainment targets) have been defined such that learning outcomes can be precisely defined. This makes it possible, in principle, to compare one course (or student, or institution) with another. This is a fundamental requirement if the services of education and training are to be offered within a competitive market which allocates resources. It enables a relative value (or rather, price) to be attached to such services.

The emphasis which this book has placed upon negotiation, and upon working from the students' current abilities and interests, makes it seem highly unlikely that such a rationalist and prescriptive approach to determining course outcomes could be useful. As the interpretive model makes clear, a large part of the teaching and learning process consists in discovering the students' interests and competences. At the beginning of a course, neither the participant nor the tutor is likely to be fully aware of these and therefore of their needs for development. Discovering what we need is as much part of the process of meeting that need in professional development as it is in psychotherapy. In this respect, professional education is quite different from normal market place activity where the customer can be assumed to have a clear idea of what they need before they make a purchase.

Beyond Technicism

So far, the notion of competences has been criticized as being a reductionist concept, and that course outcomes expressed solely in terms of such competences are likely to make the educational process inappropriately prescriptive. A further difficulty arises when we attempt to identify any competence which can be objectively measured. For example, whereas it would be easy to see how a social worker's knowledge of a procedure or technique could be objectively ascertained, it would be another matter to assess the extent to which the quality of empathy had been realized.

In general, course outcomes which are expressed exclusively in terms of technical competences (or skills) can be assessed 'objectively' in a way which fits the objectivist rationale of the market place. In doing so, however, the place of values in professional practice is denied, and wisdom is replaced by expertise.[5] Such competences are assumed to be free of a moral dimension: one can either perform a technique or not. In fact, however, this technicist approach hides a very particular moral position: one in which the professional worker, and the trainer, are conceived as being uncritical subjects. Consequently, such a view of competence disregards the very obvious fact that a professional worker may well be able to perform a particular technique, but whether or not they choose to do so in their practice will depend upon the context of values in which they work. A social worker who practices within a highly authoritarian regime, for example, may not always exercise their competence if they see this to be in the service of values which they reject. Thus, even if it were possible to describe professional practice in terms of technique (and course outcomes in terms of techniques mastered), professional development would not be assured without an engagement with the moral issues relating to the context in which practice takes place.

On the other hand, outcomes which are expressed in terms which make the moral aspects of practice explicit are inevitably much more open to interpretation. They can only be expressed, and assessed, from a position of moral values. A course description expressed in terms of such outcomes, thereby identifies a particular moral perspective which underlies the course. If we are to resist the pressure to formulate course outcomes in technical terms alone, we therefore need some way of stating them, and the competences which they serve to develop, which makes explicit the moral values upon which professional practice is based.

The temptation here is to reject the whole notion of professional competence as being an inappropriate way to think of the outcomes of professional learning. The danger with such an approach, however, is that it refuses to recognize the political power of the language of competences. Courses which refuse to engage with this language are likely to become marginalized. The alternative, is to reformulate a conception of professional competence in non-technicist terms.

In a recent study which attempts to do just this, a framework which could provide a basis for deriving the levels of non-technicist competences is suggested. Among the elements which might comprise this framework is the following statement:

> Professional work involves commitment to a specific set of moral purposes, and professional workers will recognize the inevitably complex and serious responsibilities which arise when attempting to apply ethical principles to particular cases. (see Maisch and Winter, 1991b, p. 18)

An indication of a level of competence based upon such a statement, and a description of course outcomes in relation to it, would clearly avoid the charge of technicism. Its recognition that professional work is an essentially moral activity is consistent with much of the discussion in the earlier chapters.

The 'serious responsibilities which arise when attempting to apply ethical principles to particular cases' here result from the fact that the moral purposes of professional life are often in conflict with each other. For example, while the Hippocratic Oath may be said to enshrine the physician's moral purpose in respect to the individual patient, a moral responsibility towards the health of the wider community may, in a particular case, be in conflict with it. The physician will then be on the horns of a dilemma.

In general, the moral aspect of professional work is characterized by the dilemmas which arise from potentially conflicting values. Could not this characteristic provide a basis for reconceptualizing professional competence?

Professional Dilemmas

A major source of dilemmas is brought sharply into focus by the 'market place' within which the professions operate. This market place is a set of structural arrangements concerning the allocation of resources. It is deemed (rightly or wrongly) to serve the needs of the wider community as these are expressed through political processes. Working within its constraints immediately confronts the professional worker with conflicting choices in attempting to meet the needs of the individual client within the limitations of resources imposed in the (supposed) interests of the wider community.

Often the degree of this limitation will be imposed by regulation, (for example, limits will be laid down concerning the financial benefits which may be made available to someone suffering a particular hardship). But a fundamental aspect of professional judgment involves making frequent decisions about what resources (of time and energy as well as financial) should be allocated to the individual in the knowledge that these resources are thereby denied to others. Even such an everyday decision as the length of a meeting with a particular client has to be made in the face of a moral dilemma. For we have to judge between the client's needs and the needs of others who also have a call upon us, in the knowledge that we do not have the resources to meet all those needs adequately. Unless professional workers have a questioning awareness of the moral dilemmas involved in making such decisions, their practice is likely to remain uncritical, governed more by the rule book than by the exercise of professional judgment.

The technical aspect of professional work gives rise to problems; the moral aspect gives rise to dilemmas. Inasmuch as this book has been concerned to emphasize the moral aspects of professional life, it would therefore be appropriate to consider the outcomes of courses in terms of raising awareness of professional dilemmas. The question to address then would be: how can the relevant professional dilemmas be identified?

One strategy might be to analyze accounts which professional people give of occasions in their working life ('critical incidents') when they have had to confront important moral dilemmas.[6] Through such accounts one could, perhaps, build up a list of professional dilemmas.[7] Awareness of these dilemmas could then be amongst the course outcomes and the ability to act with that awareness could form a basis for describing the competences which the course aimed to develop.

The problem with deriving competences, in terms of moral dilemmas, from accounts of 'critical incidents' is that we first have to decide whose accounts should be analyzed. The dilemmas which face a newly qualified professional worker will be different from those faced by an old hand. It cannot be assumed, however, that the more experienced worker is necessarily the more competent. And until a notion of competence is established, one is not in a position to select the most competent workers whose accounts of practice are to be analyzed. There is thus a circularity in any strategy for deriving a list of competences from the practice of people deemed to be competent before the analysis has got under way.

The circularity involved here could be side-stepped by analyzing the practice of those who are generally deemed to be 'experienced' and 'professionally respected' in order to arrive at a set of moral purposes relating to their practice. There would, however, be something fundamentally conservative about such a process. Established professional values would become enshrined in a framework of competences which relied too heavily upon accepted practice and doctrine. Innovative approaches to practice, developed in the face of newly identified dilemmas, would not readily become established as competences, since they would not be already established in the reportoire of the more generally respected practitioner. Courses whose outcomes were described in terms of such competences might help to pass on the accepted values of the profession, but may be ill equipped to offer any critique of these values.

The introduction of a more market oriented economy to the 'caring' professions is only one of the features of a 'post-modern'[8] society in which the moral bases of professional action are increasingly problematic and contradictory. Concerns for excellence are contradicted by concerns for equality; centralization by local autonomy; individual client centred practice by nationally regulated standards, and so on. In this dynamic and even chaotic[9] context it would seem that such a static notion of moral purposes as can be derived from experienced practitioners would be severely limiting. In the kind of advanced professional courses which are the context for this book, we should be encouraging our students to question and move beyond the limits of accepted notions of practice and thereby confront issues and dilemmas which may challenge received notions of moral purpose.

Critical Communities and Reflective Practice

If course outcomes are to be expressed in terms of the professional dilemmas which are likely to be encountered, how else can they be identified and developed? The earlier discussion on the course booklet suggests how an account of them might be based upon the experience of previous courses. This is certainly valuable. But to rely for insight solely upon the experience of past courses would be open to the same criticism of circularity and conservatism as relying upon the analysis of the practice of selected 'experienced' professionals in order to derive competences. Research into practice must be based upon past practice, but it must also look forward to develop it.

Viewing course outcomes, and the competences with which they are associated, in terms of dilemmas places reflection at the centre of professional ability. In contrast to technical competence or skill mastery (such as are defined in National Vocational Qualifications), the process of reflection never completely achieves its object. Reflection upon practice develops the ability to make judgments in the face of moral dilemmas. But it can never *solve* them, for, unlike technical problems, dilemmas are insoluble. Reflection is thus an ongoing process. As far as professional development is concerned, what is important here is to understand this as being a social process rather than merely an individual one. Such reflection must therefore take place within a community in which the participants view themselves as enquirers who are prepared to share their reflections and be open to mutual criticism within a supportive framework.

Action researchers have emphasized the central role of such a 'critical community' in professional development (Carr and Kemmis, 1986). This book has explored some of the dilemmas in attempting to make the professional course such a community. The course is, however, only a temporary experience. Shared understandings are developed, but one group of participants is soon replaced by the next. If enquiring tutors (like other professional workers) are to develop their awareness of the dilemmas which are faced in practice they must have access to longer-term critical communities within the context of their own professions.

The development of such communities amongst professional educators is a project for the enquiring tutor. An important outcome of the professional course is to sow the seeds amongst the students for them to grow critical communities in their workplaces. For it is within these, where the conflicting moral demands of practice are experienced and reflected upon, that critical understandings of professional competence can be developed and emerge in practice.

The ends of professional development then become the means.

Notes

1   Changing financial structures are claimed to make students behave more like 'consumers' than 'beneficiaries' of the system in a project report commissioned by the Employment Department from the Unit for the Development of Adult Continuing Education. See Otter (1992) p. 3.
2   The effect of such a consumerist philosophy on higher education practice is explored in Herbst (1973) pp. 58–74.
3   The case for people to have the right to 'defensive behaviour' is convincingly made in Harrison (1962).
4   For an example of a course booklet which describes the course discussed in chapter 4, see Rowland (1991b).
5   I am here using the Aristotelean concept of practical wisdom which is firmly rooted in values. For an explanation of this see Taylor (1955), pp. 97–100.

6   For a brief outline of how teachers' accounts of the critical incidents they have experienced can be analysed to ascertain the moral dilemmas faced, see Winter (1982).

7   See Maisch and Winter (1991a) where the analysis of critical incidents is further applied in relation to social work practice.

8   For an account of the postmodern condition and its economic roots, see Harvey (1989).

9   This chaotic feature of post-modern society is also reflected in the domains of mathematics and science in a number of popular books which have followed the work of Prigogine and Stengers (1984).

References

BARTHES, R. (1977) *Image — Music — Text* (trans HEATH, S.), Glasgow, Fontana/Collins.

BLIGH, D., JAQUES, D. and WARREN PIPER, D. (1975) *Seven Decisions When Teaching Students*, Exeter, University of Exeter.

BORMANN, E.G. (1990) *Small Group Communication*, New York, Harper & Row.

BOUD, D. and LUBLIN, J. (1982) 'Student self-assessment' in SQUIRES, G. (Ed) *Innovation Through Recession*, Guildford, SRHE.

BRUNER, J.S. (1966) *Toward a Theory of Instruction*, Cambridge, MA, Harvard University Press.

CANTOR, N. (1953) *The Teaching-Learning Process*, New York, Rinehart and Winston.

CARR, W. (1987) 'What is educational practice', *Journal of Philosophy of Education*, 21, 2.

CARR, W. (Ed) (1989) *Quality in Teaching*, Lewes, Falmer Press.

CARR, W. and KEMMIS, S. (1986) *Becoming Critical*, Lewes, Falmer Press.

COX, C.B. and DYSON, A.E. (Eds) (1969) *Black Paper Two*, London, The Critical Quarterly Society.

DE BEAUVOIR, S. (1946) 'Litterature et metaphysique', *Les Temps Modernes*.

DEPARTMENT OF EDUCATION AND SCIENCE (1978) *Primary Education in England*, London, HMSO.

DILLON, J.T. (1978) 'Using questions to depress student thought', *School Review*, 23.

EGAN, G. (1975) *The Skilled Helper*, California, Wadsworth.

ELLIOTT, J. (1981) *Action-Research: A Framework for Self-evaluation in Schools*, Norwich, University of East Anglia.

ELTON, L. and PARTINGTON, P. (1991) *Teaching Standards and Excellence in Higher Education*, Sheffield, CVCP Universities' Staff Development and Training Unit.

FLANDERS, N. (1970) *Analyzing Teacher Behavior*, Reading, MA, Addison Wesley.

FREIRE, P. (1972) *Pedagogy of the Oppressed*, London, Penguin.

GALTON, M., SIMON, B. and CROLL, P. (1980) *Inside the Primary Classroom*, London, Routledge & Kegan Paul.

GAMSON, Z. and ASSOCIATES (1984) *Liberating Education*, San Francisco, CA, Jossey-Bass.

GEERTZ, C. (1973) *The Interpretation of Cultures: Selected Essays*, New York, Basic Books.

GIBBS, G. (1988) *Learning by Doing*, London, FEU.

GIBBS, G. (1989) *Assessment* (Module 3), Oxford, Oxford Centre for Staff Development.

GIBSON, R. (1986) *Critical Theory and Education*, London, Hodder & Stoughton.

GREEN, M. (1973) *Teacher as Stranger*, California, Wadsworth.

GREENE, M. (Ed.) (1969) *Knowing and Being: Essays by Michael Polanyi*, London, Routledge & Kegan Paul.

GUEST, J. (1986) 'Preface' to GOLDBERG, M. (Ed) *Writing Down the Bones*, London, Shambhala.

HABERMAS, J. (1974) *Theory and Practice* (trans VIERSAL, J.), London, Heinemann.

HAMILTON, D., JENKINS, D., KING, C., MCDONALD, B. and PARLETT, M. (Eds) (1977) *Beyond the Numbers Games*, London, Macmillan.

HARRE, P. and SECORD, P.F. (1972) *The Explanation of Social Behaviour*, Oxford, Blackwell.

HARRISON, R. (1962) 'Defenses and the need to know', *Human Relations Training News*, 6, 4.

HARTLEY, J. and CAMERON, A. (1967) 'Some observations on the efficiency of lecturing', *Educational Review*, 20.

HARVEY, D. (1989) *The Post-modern Condition*, Oxford, Blackwell.

HARVEY, J.B. (1971) 'Critique of thought reform: East vs west', *Training in Business and Industry*, 8, 11.

HERBST, P. (1973) 'Work, labour and university education' in PETERS, R.S. (Ed) *The Philosophy of Education*, London, Oxford University Press.

HOLT, J. (1965) *How Children Fail*, New York, Pitman.

HOLT, J. (1967) *How Children Learn*, New York, Pitman.

JARVIS, P. (1983) *Professional Education*, London, Croom Helm.

JOURARD, S.M. (1967) 'Fascination: A phenomenological perspective on independent learning' in GLEASON, G.T. (Ed) *The Theory and Nature of Independent Learning*, Scranton, PA, International Textbook Co.

KELMAN, H.C. (1965) 'Manipulation of human behaviour: An ethical dilemma for the social scientist', *Journal of Social Issues*, 21, 2.

LABOV, W. (1970) *The Study of Non-standard English*, Washington, DC, National Council of Teachers of English.

MCKERNAN, J. (1991) *Curriculum Action Research*, London, Kogan Page.

MAISCH, M. and WINTER, R. (1991a) *The Asset Programme Papers, Volume II: The Development and Assessment of Professional Competences*, Chelmsford, Anglia Polytechnic/Essex Social Services Department.

MAISCH, M. and WINTER, R. (1991b) *The Asset Programme Papers, Volume I:*

Professionalism and Competence, Chelmsford, Anglia Polytechnic/Essex Social Services Department.

MASSON, J. (1989) *Against Therapy*, London, Fontana.

MURDOCH, I. (1965) *Sartre*, Cambridge, Bowes & Bowes.

OTTER, S. (1992) *Learning Outcomes in Higher Education*, London, Employment Department.

PARLETT, M. and HAMILTON, D. (1977) 'Evaluation as illumination' in HAMILTON, D., JENKINS, D., KING, C., McDONALD, B. and PARLETT, M. (Eds) (1977) *Beyond the Numbers Games*, London, Macmillan.

PERLS, F.S. (1969) *Gestalt Therapy Verbatim*, New York, Bantam Books.

POLANYI, M. (1958) *Personal Knowledge*, London, Routledge & Kegan Paul.

POLANYI, M. (1961) 'Knowing and being' in GREENE, M. (Ed) (1969) *Knowing and Being: Essays by Michael Polanyi*, London, Routledge & Kegan Paul.

PRIGOGINE, I. and STENGERS, I. (1984) *Order out of Chaos: Man's New Dialogue with Nature*, London, Fontana Paperback.

RADLEY, A. (1980) 'Student learning as social practice' in SALMON, P. (Ed) *Coming to Know*, London, Routledge & Kegan Paul.

ROGERS, C. (1977) *Carl Rogers on Personal Power*, London, Constable.

ROSKIN, R. (1976) *Learning by Experience*, Bradford, MCB Monographs.

ROWAN, J. (1990) *Sub-personalities: The People Inside Us*, London, Routledge.

ROWLAND, G., ROWLAND, S. and WINTER, R. (1990) 'Writing fiction as enquiry into professional practice', *Journal of Curriculum Studies*, 22, 3.

ROWLAND, S. (1984) *The Enquiring Classroom*, Lewes, Falmer Press.

ROWLAND, S. (1991a) 'The power of silence', *British Educational Research Journal*, 17, 2.

ROWLAND, S. (1991b) *The Adult's Curriculum: Explorations in Active Learning*, Sheffield, University of Sheffield.

ROWNTREE, D. (1986) *Teaching Through Self Instruction*, London, Kogan Page/ Nichols.

RUDDUCK, J. (1978) *Learning Through Small Group Discussion*, Guildford, Research into Higher Education.

RUDDUCK, J. and HOPKINS, D. (1985) *Research as a Basis for Teaching: Readings from the Work of Lawrence Stenhouse*, London, Heinemann.

SARTRE, J.-P. (1963) *Nausea* (trans BALDICK, R.), London, Penguin.

SCHON, D. (1983) *The Reflective Practitioner*, London, Temple Smith.

SCHON, D. (1987) *Educating the Reflective Practitioner*, San Francisco, CA, Jossey-Bass.

TAYLOR, A.E. (1955) *Aristotle*, New York, Dover Publications.

THOMPSON, J.B. and HELD, D. (Eds) (1982) *Habermas: Critical Debates*, London, Macmillan.

VAN MANEN, M. (1989) 'The relation between research and pedagogy' in PINAR, W.F. (Ed) *Contemporary Curriculum Discourses*, Arizona, Gorsuch Scarisbrook.

WALKER, R. (1981) 'On the uses of fiction in educational research — (and I don't mean Cyril Burt)' in SMETHERTON, D. (Ed) *Practising Evaluation*, Driffield, Nafferton Books.

WALTER, G.A. and MARKS, S.E. (1981) *Experiential Learning and Change*, New York, John Wiley & Sons.

WARNER WEIL, S. and McGILL, I. (1989) *Making Sense of Experiential Learning*, London, Oxford University Press.

WILLIS, G. (Ed) (1978) *Qualitative Evaluation*, California, McCutchan Publication Corporation.

WINTER, R. (1982) 'Dilemma analysis', *Cambridge Journal of Education*, 12, 3.

WINTER, R. (1989) *Learning from Experience*, Lewes, Falmer Press.